The Pacific Century
Second Edition
Study Guide

The Pacific Century
Second Edition
Study Guide

Pauletta Otis

Routledge
Taylor & Francis Group
LONDON AND NEW YORK

First published 1999 by Westview Press

Published 2019 by Routledge
52 Vanderbilt Avenue, New York, NY 10017
2 Park Square, Milton Park, Abingdon, Oxon OX14 4RN

Routledge is an imprint of the Taylor & Francis Group, an informa business

Copyright © 1999 by Taylor & Francis

All rights reserved. No part of this book may be reprinted or reproduced or utilised in any form or by any electronic, mechanical, or other means, now known or hereafter invented, including photocopying and recording, or in any information storage or retrieval system, without permission in writing from the publishers.

Notice:
Product or corporate names may be trademarks or registered trademarks, and are used only for identification and explanation without intent to infringe.

A CIP catalog record for this book is available from the Library of Congress.

ISBN 13: 978-0-367-29464-9 (hbk)
ISBN 13: 978-0-367-31010-3 (pbk)

TABLE OF CONTENTS

INTRODUCTION

CHAPTER 1: Dynasties, Empires and Ages of Commerce	5
CHAPTER 2: Seaborne Barbarians: Incursions by the West	13
CHAPTER 3: Meiji: Japan in the Age of Imperialism	21
CHAPTER 4: The Rise of Nationalism and Communism	29
CHAPTER 5: Maelstrom: the Pacific War and its Aftermath	41
CHAPTER 6: Miracle by Design: The Postwar Renaissance	49
CHAPTER 7: The New Asian Capitalists	59
CHAPTER 8: Power, Authority, and the Advent of Democracy	69
CHAPTER 9: Sentimental Imperialists: America in Asia	79
CHAPTER 10: China's March to Modernization	87
CHAPTER 11: Beyond the Revolution: Indonesia and Vietnam	95
CHAPTER 12: Siberian Salient: Russia in Pacific Asia	103
CHAPTER 13: Pacific Century: Regional and Global Perspectives	109

INTRODUCTION

Overview

The twentieth century is the Pacific Century. This century has been characterized as one of profound change brought about by modernization, democratization, and economic integration of Asia with the rest of the world. One of the major concerns of the text is to provide basic information and analysis concerning how the forces of change during this period will provide a base for the future of the region.

Part of the problem in studying an area of the world is defining exactly where and what that definition includes and excludes. The term "Pacific Basin" is the most inclusive as it refers to all countries or regions which touch on the Pacific Ocean. "Pacific Asia" is a more restrictive definition as it generally excludes the Americas and the Indian subcontinent. The term "Asia" was originally used by outsiders to refer to any region "not European." All of the definitions are fluid and variously refer to geographic regions, populations, cultures, or political units.

Outline

I. Importance and theme of the text
    A. Relevance to the region and the rest of the world
    B. Effects of modernization
    C. Conceptual clarification
        1. Area is defined in fluid, self-identifying and reflective terms
        2. Differences in geographical, political, and historical terminology

II. Regions defined
    A. East Asia
        1. China
            a. Manchuria
            b. Mongolia
            c. Xinjiang
            d. Tibet
            e. Taiwan
        2. Korean, Japan, and Eastern Siberia
    B. Southeast Asia
        1. Vietnam, Laos, Cambodia, Thailand
        2. Islands of S.E. Asia
            a. Malaysia
            b. Indonesia
    C. Oceania
        1. Australia
        2. New Zealand
        3. Pacific islands
    D. North America

III. Two centers of gravity
    A. The Pacific islands - the ocean
    B. The Great Wall - the land mass

Key Terms

Asia
Pacific Asia
Pacific Basin

Place Names

East Asia: China, Korea, Japan
South East Asia: Vietnam, Laos, Cambodia, Thailand, Malaysia, Indonesia
Oceania: Australia, New Zealand, and the Pacific Islands

Key Concepts

Pacific Century: the twenty-first century noted for a renewal of force and dynamism in the Pacific region.

Pacific transition: in this text, transition refers to a relatively rapid change from tradiitional or inward-turning, regional interests to emerging social, political, and economic global modernization.

Pacific Basin: those countries whose borders rim the Pacific Ocean or whose political life is determined in large measure by continguity with the Pacific Ocean.

land-centered definitions: conceptual inclusiveness of politically organized units based on land or the use of land by human beings.

ocean-centered definitions: conceptual inclusiveness of politically organized units that rely on oceans for the central configuration.

Chronology: measurement of time in regular divisions or sequences and assigning events to their proper dates.

Knowledge, understanding, and evaluation

1. The focus of this study is the Asian Pacific.

2. The time frame is the twentieth century: 1900 to 2000CE

3. There are several major themes:

    (A) The relationship between economic and political development

    (B) U.S. foreign policy in the Pacific

    (C) The unique experience of each of the Asian countries.

    (D) Commonalities in the experiences of each of the countries.

    (E) The question of whether there is a clash of cultures between East and West or whether the Asian experience is simply another aspect of a more general and universal human experience.

HINTS:

1. Keep a map book and time lines as handy reference tools. Refer to them periodically to help sort out the large amount of material covered in this text.

2. Look through the text for the charts and graphs which have been included. They are interesting and will be very helpful in future study and understanding. Reference the Time Chart on pages 11-15.

3. This text (and related course work) covers a huge land area, over a long period of time with an extraordinary number of complex factors. This means that it is to some degree intensely dissatisfying because a single text cannot delve deeply into any single subject. It is sincerely hoped that this overview will impel and entice a student to want to know more about specific cases.

CHAPTER 1

Dynasties, Empires and Ages of Commerce:
Pacific Asia to the Nineteenth Century

Overview

This chapter provides a general chronological development of the civilizations and empires in this region and provides a basic framework for understanding the schools of thought which provided the ideological bases for those civilizations and empires. The authors begin with a broad overview of the development of the first Chinese Empire. They then relate the unique experiences of Korea, Japan, and the islands to their own indigenous conditions and to the larger region.

In China, Qin Shihuandgdi named himself the first emperor and began the **Qin** (Ch'in) Dynasty with related laws, bureaucracy, and military forces. The philosophical basis for his rule was the idea that the Emperor's role and person had inherent power and virtue. The Emperor, or Son of Heaven, was supreme arbiter between Heaven and Earth. Burning books to be rid of all the alternative viewpoints, he established a pattern of promotion of an acceptable "party line." The optimistic Confucianists were attacked by the Legalists who believed that governments should be based on strict rules. They established a counter force and essentially backed the existence of the totalitarian state. The Daoists took another position: they basically supported the idea that a basic harmony would exist if individuals followed a natural course, or the Way. In relationship to governance, these ideas are congruent with what would be later identified as "grass-roots" or popular movements - reform of government by individuals and maintenance of governance by the proper behavior of individual citizens and natural economic forces.

The **Han** Dynasty is associated with the establishment of a universally understood written Chinese language. This allowed a governing structure for the Chinese state that held sway for nearly two thousand years: an absolute monarch, a council of ministers, and a civil service. During this period, Wei Man invaded the area of Korea and founded the kingdom of Chosun (194 BCE). Also during this time, the Wa (Japanese) broke a pattern of self-imposed isolation, and invaded Korea. Although in cultural contact with China and other countries in the region and incorporated some aspects of Confucianism and Buddhism, the Japanese maintained their distinctive Shinto beliefs. This supported the idea that while the origin of imperial authority may be "heaven," the mandate was changing and in response to elite manipulation. In the seventh century, a Japanese delegation to China brought back ideas that formed the basis for the Taika Reform that supported the increasing centralization of state authority. Korea was unified when the Silla overthrew the Paekche in 668 allowing it to develop relatively unhindered by outside aggression.

The **Tang** Dynasty established a Tributary system for external relationships. Internally the period is characterized by the aristocratic maintenance of rule and a period of relative prosperity supported by a new merchant class. The Indian connection with Buddhism (as accepted in a variety of culturally specific ways) had an enormous effect on China, Japan, and Korea in systems of artistic endeavor, philosophy, and political rule. The dynasty failed as the Han dynasty when expenses out-weighed revenue.

The **Song** dynasty established its legitimacy on the commercial growth of the Hangzi Valley, particularly Canton and Quanzhou. Trade with Korea, Arabia, Persia, India, and as far away as Constantinople, supported a rich trading economy and new cultural developments. In this atmosphere Zhuxi (Chu Hsi, 1130-1200) encouraged the spread of Neo-Confucianism to the masses.

In 1206, Genghis Khan's disciplined army of 130,000 men drove the northern Song Chinese southward. The **Monguls** did not conquer the Southern Song until 1260 when Kublai became the Great Khan. He extended the Mongol khanates to Korea and other land based civilizations, but failed in naval excursions against Japan and Java. (This is the era of the *kamikazi* or "divine wind" associated with the defeat of the Mongols by the samurai on the island of Kyushu.) This is also the era of Marco Polo's visit, the establishment of Christian missions, and a suggested alliance of China, Persia, and the Europeans against the Saracens of the Middle East.

The **Ming** dynasty (1368-1644) with its capital of Nanjing provided prolonged period of peace and stability for China based on successful trade relationships in the region. It is a period known for the successes of the Chinese armada of 20,000 men aboard an estimated 316 ships which supported Chinese commerce in Pacific Asia. Tributary relationship with surrounding countries were generally peaceful although China's relationship with Korea was constantly strained. Korea was forced to accept the "younger brother" or *yi* designation admitting its inferior status. The Ming dynasty came apart as the result of several factors: internal corruption, expenditures on defense systems and irrigation projects, international fall of the price of silver, attack of Korean by the Yokugawa Shoguns of Japan, and the persistent and pervasive influence of foreign learning.

The **Manchus** led by Nurhachi attacked the Ming in 1618. This empire which lasted until 1911 was resistant to change. Its policies and practices were to leave China vulnerable to both internal and foreign influence. One of the most significant precursors of the twentieth century revolutionary changes, was the Taiping Rebellion of 1851-1864. The domestic grievances based on overwhelming poverty, class distinctions, urbanization, and lack of government responsiveness were coupled with new ideologies brought in by the Europeans. This formed a lethal mixture of reality problems and ideological based solutions.

Among the religions or schools of thought most important to this region are Confucianism, Legalism, Daoism, Islam and Christianity. Each provided an intellectual framework for related economic and political organization.

Confucius (Kong Fuzi, 551-479 BCI) emphasized orderliness based on mutual responsibility. The Legalists, referring to the era of Sage Kings, supported elite maintenance of social order. Lao Tzu and the Daoists saw orderliness as a process, or Way. The ideologies of the twentieth century - Democracy, Communism, and Maoism - have historic predecessors in these philosophies.

Turning to Southeast Asia, the authors discuss continuity and change in each of the countries of the region with special attention given to Cambodia, Vietnam, and the Philippines. The Khmer empire of Angkor and the Srivijayan Empire of Sumatra were especially important. The Vietnamese experience was unique in that although it was subject to heavy influence from China, it became independent as early as 939 A.D. and remained a separate entity from that period. The Southeast Asian experience was influenced by the geography and climate of the region which supported rice, forests, and sea lanes. Indigenous practices were influenced by the powerful northern neighbor, China and even more importantly, India. Buddhism was especially significant. The fifteenth to the seventeenth century was a period known as the "age of commerce" in which maritime links were particularly significant. These supported religious and cultural as well as economic interaction. In the 19th century, the major forces for change were those related to economic development and modernization: commerce, urbanization, religious movements, education and popular literacy, the formation of the modern state system, and various economic factors.

By the beginning of the twentieth century, the countries and regions of Asia had established continuity of culture, political patterns, and social organization based on the uniquely Asian experience. These were to come under conditions of rapid change in the next century.

Outline

I.   China dynasties
      A.   Qin (Ch'in)
      B.   Han
      C.   Tang
      D.   Song

        E.   Monguls
        F.   Ming
        G.   Manchu
II.   South East Asia
        A.   Importance of geography and climate
        B.   Influence of China and India
        C.   Contributions of Buddhism, Islam, and Christianity
        D.   Historical kingdoms
             1.   The Khmer
             2.   Srivijayan of Sumatra
        E.   Unique experience of Vietnam
        F.   Unique experience of Philippines
III. Stage set for twentieth century
        A.   Asian continuity of culture, political patterns, and social organization
        B.   The nineteenth century was a period of change related to economic development and modernization
        C.   The twentieth century would be a period related to political change and integration with the rest of the world

Key Terms

inflected language
Shang people
Daoism
Confucianism
Legalism
Buddhism
Islam
Mandate of Heaven

bakufu kamikazi
shoguns
Chosun kingdom
"Wa"
Silla
Mahayana Buddhism
Theravada Buddhism
Bushido

Names	Places	Dates
Lao Tzu	Huang He River	245 BCE
Confucius	Yangtze River	1231
Qin Shihuangdi	Manchurian Plain	
Li Si	Malacca Strait	
Lady Murasaki	Vietnam	
Shikibu	Angkor Wat	
Ghengis Khan	Sumatra	
Kublai Khan	Cambodia	
Marco Polo	Thailand	
Minamoto Yoritomo	Laos	
Wei Man	Burma	
Siddhartha		

Key Concepts

<u>dynasty</u>: a family or group which maintains power over several generations

<u>sage king</u>: early rulers of China who are said to have had both wisdom and authority

<u>mandate of heaven</u>: human rulers who had been given special qualities making them supreme arbiters between Heaven and Earth.

<u>long walls</u>: walls built on the perimeter of Chinese empires used to defend borders

<u>small states</u>: in the Asian context, this term refers to kingdoms, principalities and sultanates that are small in size, limited in political importance, but that maintain independent sovereignty

<u>maritime cities</u>: cities built along coastlines that are dependent on seaborne commerce

theocratic rule: government which takes as its legitimizing premise the authority of divine sanction

rice and fish economy: a basic, rural dependence on basic food stuffs implying lack of a money dependent economy

Indianized: in the Asian context, this refers to the spread of Hindu and Buddhist culture into the Asian cultural arena; especially important in mythology, art forms, and other religious artifacts

Sinitic: refering to 'sino' or Chinese

Knowledge, understanding, and evaluation

1. Know each of the major periods in the dynastic history of China: Qin, Han, Three Kingdoms, Six Dynasties, Sui, Tang, Song, Yuan, Ming and Manchu.

2. Understand the relationship of a written language to the development of a bureaucratic state.

3. Understand that the dynamic relationship between order and disorder is manifested in the basic political organization of any society. The Asian philosophers and political authorities struggled with this understanding for centuries. Be able to discuss or even debate the proposition that the Legalists may base their ideas in assumptions close to those held by modern conservatives, that Confucianists may be base their assumptions on ideas which are foundational to Liberal thinking, and the Daoists are in some respects close to American populism.

4. Be able to discuss how or in what ways the history of Asia influences the present.

5. Be able to discuss how and in what ways Asian culture shapes political arrangements.

Topics for Research Papers:

Mahayana and Thiravada Buddhism
Silk Road
The Versailles Treaty and its Effect on Asian Nationalism
The City of Beijing
Kublai Khan (1215-1294)
Islam in Asia
Confucius and Mao in the Formation of Chinese Communist Ideology
The Opium Wars
The Boxer Rebellion
Comparison of Portuguese, Dutch, Spanish, French, and English Forms of Colonialism in Asia
The Srivijayan Empire
The Kymer of Angkor Wat
The Pyramids of Southeast Asia
The Maritime World of Southeast Asia: Seventeenth to the Nineteenth Century
Pirates of Southeast Asian Waterways

CHAPTER 2

Seaborne Barbarians: Incursions by the West

Overview

This chapter focuses on the relationship between Asia and Europe during the period immediately prior to the twentieth century. The commercial and colonial powers of Europe were Portugal, Spain, the Dutch, France, and England. Commercial relationships were originally based on trade goods but this soon shifted to a production base of agricultural commodities such as rubber, coffee, tin, and rice. To support this production, the Europeans believed that they should have more control over indigenous production of these goods to ensure quality control and sufficient production. This eventually led to colonialization and political domination of these areas.

The motivations of European powers varied between countries and over time. The Portuguese and Spanish were interested in both commerce and the spread of Christianity. The Dutch were singularly interested in commercial relationships as evidenced in activities of the Dutch East India Company. The French had religious, commercial and political motivation. The English shifted from the strictly commercial interests of the British East India Company to a more deregulated commercial base supported by the British Empire of the eighteenth century which controlled approximately one-fourth of the world's land surface.

Two factors are especially difficult to understand and must be analyzed in historical context: (1) the opium trade and (2) the coolie trade. The opium trade was supported by commercial interests in Britain but hotly debated in religious and political circles. It had supplanted the more valuable silver as a monetary unit of exchange. The Chinese had porcelain, silk, spices, and other commodities which the British were able buy and then sell for a profit in areas of their vast Empire. The opium grown in India was given in exchange for these commodities and this had a devastating effect on the social and commercial fabric of China. The Manchus were very well aware of the damage it was causing but unable to stop this aspect of "free trade" against the superior military power of Great Britain. The coolie trade, the buying and selling of cheap labor, was another significant problem. Chinese and other Asian laborers, unable to find work in the depressed economy of their own country, were willing to contract their services to companies which then transported them to various regions of the developing world. The conditions for these laborers was as serious as if they had been slaves. Again, the Chinese government, well aware of the problem, was unable to stop this practice. Only with the Chinese seizure of a ship flying the British flag was an incident created of enough international significance to bring the problem to world attention. Other problems included disease, environmental degradation, alcohol and firearms.

The chronology of the era begins with the fall of Constantinople to the Turks is 1453 and the closing of land routes to Asia and the opening of sea lanes. The Portuguese bought spices, silk, porcelain, ivory, sandalwood, and jewels - the commodities which China traded to other ports throughout the South China Sea and the Indian Ocean. The first Jesuits to Guangzhou arrived in 1582 led by Matteo Ricci. After the Treaty of Tordesillas (1494), the Spanish explorer Magellan arrived in the Philippines. The Dutch East Indian Company drove out the Portuguese, held back the British and dominated many of the Southeast Asian markets. After Robert Clive's victory in India (1757), the British became a dominant power in the region responsible for changing the medium of exchange from silver to opium. Russia exploited the northern areas where fur-bearing animals became over-hunted. Whalers from all countries depleted the species.

Political power and military control supported commercial activities. Each of the European groups supported the idea of extra-territoriality i.e. that European laws and customs had original jurisdiction wherever Europeans were concerned. This was both an evidence of European belief in the cultural superiority of the European races and a "clash of cultures" problem. Treaties were unequal and formed the basis for political domination of China, Vietnam, Laos, Malaysia, Indonesia, and Cambodia.

Several individuals are notable: James Brooke founded the "White Raja" dynasty in Sarawak which was paternalistic control in support of the tin trade. Robert Hart was a trusted adviser to the Quin government and supported intercultural activities which won him acclaim in both England and China. Robert Clive was an able and efficient administrator of East India. Sir Stamford Raffles was a visionary and pioneer who helped Singapore become a major regional trading center. King Mongkut and his son Chulalongkorn of Siam (Thailand) accommodated Western demands and ably manipulated the British and French.

The United States became involved when Secretary of State John Hay in the McKinley administration took the position that European competition in China would be detrimental to U.S. interests. He sent a timely diplomatic notes to all four of the major European powers supporting what he called an Open Door policy. This initiative set the tone for a future "special relationship" between China and the United States.

This period is known as a period of rapid change as influenced by commercial and political activities on the Asian landscape. During the next century, Western science, technology, and philosophy would further change the pattern, pace, and frequency of interaction with Asia.

Outline

I. Background
II. Motivations
    A. Commercial
        1. Trade

         2. Production of agricultural goods
         3. Beginnings of industrial production
      B. Colonial
         1. To support commercial production
         2. Some influence of religion
      C. Military and political
         1. In support of commercial interests
         2. In support of the extraterritoriality of European nations
III. Factors of exploitation
      A. Opium
         1. Substituted for silver
         2. Problem for both China and British public
      B. Coolie trade
         1. From China and other Southeast Asian countries
         2. To developing countries of the entire world
         3. Problem for countries exporting labor and those importing labor
         4. The Arrow War
IV. Chronology of the era
      A. From period of the fall of Constantinople and closing of land routes
      B. Portuguese trade in spices, silk, porcelain, ivory, and sandalwood
      C. Spanish compete with Portuguese
      D. Dutch East India Company supports trade and incipient agricultural production
      E. British become dominant power
V. Political and legal power and the principle of extra-territoriality
VI. Notable individuals
      A. James Brooke and the "White Raja" dynasty of Sarawak
      B. Robert Hart adviser to Chinese government
      C. Robert Clive of India
      D. Sir Stamford Raffles established Singapore as regional trading center
      E. King Mongkut and son Chulalongkorn of Siam ably

                manipulates British and French
VII.   United States involvement
        A.   John Hay's note to the four powers
        B.   Open Door policy
        C.   Basis for future U.S.' "special relationship" with China

Key Terms

barbarians	Dutch East India Company
colonialism	the Chinese "junk"
imperialism	sandalwood
silver	extraterritoriality
opium trade	"special relationship"
British East India Company	

Names	**Places**	**Dates**
Matteo Ricci	Guangzhou	First Opium War
Magellan	(Canton)	(1842)
Robert Clive	Straits of Malacca	Second Burma War
Robert Hart	Manchester	(1886)
James Brooke		Treaty of Nanjing
Sir Stamford Raffles		(1842)
King Mongkut and		The Arrow War
son Chulalongkorn		(1856)
John Hay		
Lin Zexu		
Queen Victoria		

Key Concepts

<u>imperialism</u>: the policy of extending a state's authority by territorial acquisition or by the establishment of economic and political hegemony over other polities

Westernization: term used to describe the process of a country coming under Western cultural and political influence and adopting beliefs, values and attitudes learned from the West.

modernization: the process by which a country or culture becomes industrialized and democratic. It infers progress, development, use of rationality and the scientific method and is contingent upon the values which support change.

extraterritoriality: the idea that the laws of a country can be applied to its citizens who are physically present in other sovereign states.

foreign concessions: parcels of land ceded to foreign powers in Chinese cities. In these areas (such as Shanghai), the foreign power assumed the right of sovereign jurisdiction

Orientals: In European thinking, the term Oriental referred to peoples and cultures that were not specifically European, Arab, African, nor American, i.e., any group residing between the western borders of the Ottoman Empire and the Pacific Ocean.

casus belli: a formal, legal cause for declaring war.

unequal treaty: treaties between and among states wherein the balance of power is disproportionately held by one of the signatories

coolie trade: the buying and selling of human labor (kangani system) prevalent through South Asia and the Pacific during the seventeenth and eighteenth centuries.

steam driven commerce: the advent of coal powered sailing vessels which made coal a necessary and desired commodity

Knowledge, understanding, and evaluation

1. The major agricultural export products of Asia during this period were rubber, coffee, tin, and rice.

2. The major colonial powers were Portugal, Dutch, Spain, France, and England. Be able to trace the influence of each of these powers in specific areas of Asia.

3. Be able to discuss the authors' contention that colonialism followed commerce.

4. Evaluate opium trade as a moral, political and economic problem of the era and compare it to the twentieth century drug wars.

5. Imperialism had both economic and political foundations.

Topics for Research Papers

The Fall of Constantinople and the Consequences for Asia
Opium Trade as Free Market Capitalism
Robert Clive of India
The Purchase of Human Labor: Comparing Slavery and Coolie Practices
The Open-Door Policy
The "White Raja" of Sarawak
Singapore and Hong Kong in Comparison
Comparing the Dutch East India Company and the British East India Company
The United States and its Special Relationship with China
The Chinese and the Building of U.S. Railroads
The Laying of the Pacific Transcontinental Telegraph Cables
French Colonial Policy in Vietnam
The King of Siam
The History of Piracy in the South Pacific
The Arrow War

CHAPTER 3

Meiji: Japan in the Age of Imperialism

Overview

This chapter covers the period between the 'opening of Japan' by Commodore Perry and the Emperor Meiji's death in 1912. The discussion centers on Japan's Meiji transformation which was based on technological advancement, consolidation of the modern nation-state, popular participation in government, capitalism, commercial trade, and high levels of social energy.

In the early part of the period the Japanese Shogan was besieged by both domestic and international pressures for change. The coming of Commodore Perry's black ships signaled the end of the one era and the beginning of another. A combination of pressure from domestic forces (the *daimyo* (feudal lords) and samurai most notably) and the realization that Japan would suffer the same fate as China if it did not change dramatically, led to a series of domestic consequences. The government became more centralized under the symbolism provided by Emperor Mutsuhito and correspondingly allowed more autonomous action by the samurai and local constituencies thereby supplanting *daimyo* control. An innovative solution was found to reform the land-tax system. The new tax did not increase the amount collected under the Tokugawa and the tax become uniform throughout the island. These measures were pragmatic, seemed just and were eminently acceptable to the populace. Unlike the philosophical underpinnings prevalent in China at the time, Japanese samurai contributed a operating strategies based on energy, progress, and pragmatism. Both education and the family remained core to the values of the society. Most importantly these provided a social foundation to industrial organization. The *Zaibatsu* such as Mitsubishi, Sumitomo, Yasuda would become key to the future transformation of Japan to an increasingly important economic and military power. The Meiji Constitution and the formation of the Diet mirrored the changes in the social and economic spheres allow both enhanced participation and communication alongside enhanced centralization of decision and policy making.

At the same time, China was experiencing social upheaval and fragmentation. The Taiping Rebellion (1850-1864) was particularly troublesome and the stage was set for future peasant uprisings. An exception to the corruption and ineptitude shown in the court of Empress Dowager Cixi, was the military commander, Li Hongzhang and his incorruptible and efficient administration of the northern provinces of China.

Korea was to become the fulcrum between the declining power of the Chinese empire and the rising power of the Japanese. As the Korean elites suffered the same "culture shock" as was found in China and Japan, events took a slightly different turn. The philosophy of *Tonghak* as promulgated by Ch'oe Che-u was a popularist, messianic movement. The final result was the fall of the imperial court and the establishment of a popular, democratic government. These factors became temporarily overshadowed by the power competition of regional players - Russia, China and Japan which used Korea as a staging ground for their military confrontation. The Japanese obliterated the Russian fleet in a surprise attack on Port Arthur. What followed this "liberation" of Korea was the supplanting of one imperial power (Russia) with another (Japan). Koreans still cite the Nanjing Massacre as evidence of Japanese imperial intentions. The military success of Japan had important consequences for the region. It demonstrated that European powers could be fought and that battles could be won by Asians using Asian ideas and European technologies. This provided implicit proof of Asian cultural superiority and was to have devastating effect in the next fifty years. Ironically, however, much of the devastation of military excursions was felt by other Asian people - specifically the Koreans and Chinese.

Outline

I. The Shogun's dilemma
    A. Internal pressures
        1. Daimyo
        2. Imperial Court and the Mikado
        3. Samurai
    B. External pressures
        1. Example of domination of China by foreigners
        2. Mission to Europe and U.S. in 1862
    C. Choices
        1. Close Japan to outsiders; control direct intervention
        2. Open Japan to new ideas, technologies, commerce, and education

II. Major domestic changes
    A. Centralization and control by the government; use of emperor as symbol
    B. Political decentralization and autonomy; suppression of *daimyo* influence
    C. Land-tax reform
    D. Support for universal education and conscription
    E. Role of the samurai in economic development encouraged pragmatism
    F. Establishment of the Diet and the Meiji Constitution

III. Regional influences
    A. China
        1. Taiping Rebellion (1850-1864)
        2. Li Hongzhang
        3. Corruption and the rule of Empress Dowager Cixi
    B. Korea
        1. As fulcrum between China and Japan
        2. The beginning of "Eastern ethics and Western science" philosophy
            a. *Tonghak*
            b. *Ch'oe Che-u*

3. The court and Queen Min
4. Opening by Japan in 1873 and Treaty of Kanghwa (1876)
5. Sino-Japanese War
    a. China signs Li-Lobanov Treaty with Russia
    b. Boxer Rebellion in China
6. The Kabo Reform of 1894 and King Kojong
C. Russo-Japanese War (1904)
    1. Surprise naval attack on Port Arthur and obliteration of Russian fleet
    2. Demonstration effect for other Asian countries
    3. Nanjing Massacre

IV. Key points
A. Japan overtakes China during this period
    1. Result of foreign dominant of China - size and complexity
    2. Philosophical emphasis in China; pragmatic Samurai emphasis in Japan
B. Individualism does not become dominant
C. The *Zaibatsu* such as Mitsubishi, Sumitomo, Yasuda become key to future events
D. Similar social forces in Europe based on ideas of achievement, self-expression, industry

Key Terms

daimyo
sonnojoi
mikado
Diet
shogun
Treaty of Kanagawa (1858)

Emperor Mutsuhito
Meiji Constitution
Tonghak
Massacre of Nanjing

Names
Townsend Harris
Empress Dowager Cixi
Li Hongzhang
Fulizawa Yukichi
Emperor Meiji
Queen Min

Dates,
(Perry) 8 July 1853
1894 Sino-Japanese War
1904 Russo-Japanese War

Places
Port Arthur
Nanjing

Key Concepts

yellow peril: a popular term that referred to the perceived menace that the Chinese and Japanese presented to the West, both in Asia and at home

Western learning (sohak): first used to refer to Roman Catholicism and later to Western science

Manifest Destiny: the doctrine that God had given a special inheritance to the country associated and had both the right and duty to take enlightenment to foreign regions. Used to support territorial and cultural imperialism.

receptivity: term used to refer to the degree of cultural openness to new ideas and technologies legitimacy: the degree to which a government reflects the needs and wishes of its citizenry. It is assumed that democracy is the most legitimate of governmental forms.

business conglomerates (zaibatsu): cooperation and networking between various businesses and government

anachronism: something out of place or unsuited to its time

undeclared war: hostilities between political units without governmental prior notification. Recommended in the teachings of Sun Tsu.

idealists: visionary or one whose conduct is influenced by a set of ideals held in relationship to perfection

extremists: those individuals who take out of the ordinary measures to support a particular belief system or ideology

Knowledge, understanding, and evaluation

1. Understand the nature of the relationship between ideology and political organization and be able to discuss how this relationship became apparent in China and Japan.

2. Understand that the "opening" of Japan was actually a "reopening." Japan had a tradition of cultural and technological learning from other countries.

3. Be able to explain why and how Japan's transition from the Tokugawa era to Meiji era was accomplished without violence and revolution.

4. Understand that capitalism is not dependent on individualism.

5. The *zaibatsu* organization is not a plot to keep foreigners out, but a system meant to keep Japanese people, goods and services "in."

6. Korean history has been reflective of the requirements and aspirations of regional powers.

7. Education and literacy were and continue to be basic to cultural change and political development.

8. Know that there were oppositionary forces in all of the events during this era. For example, the corrupt existed along with the incorruptible; the revolutionary alongside the reactionary; and the individual within the society. It is drastic oversimplification to assume that "all Japanese" or "all Chinese" believed/ behaved the same way.

9. Both the Meiji Constitution and the Korean Constitution were remarkable documents and very much in keeping with the Western liberal tradition.

10. Be able to explain why and how Japan was able to overtake China as a regional power during this period.

Topics for Research Papers

The Political and Economic Effects of Whaling in the Pacific
The Samurai Influence on Japanese Industry
The Story of C. G. "Chinese" Gordon
F. T. Ward of Salem, Massachusetts
The Taiping Rebellion
The Boxer Rebellion
Eastern Ethics and Western Science
The Massacre of Nanjing
The Russo-Japanese War
The Sino-Japanese War
Tokyo in 1890 as a Place of Refuge for Future Revolutionary Leaders
The History of the Zaibatsu
Li Hongzhang
Catholicism in Korean 1880-1910
Tonghak: Political or Religious Movement?

CHAPTER 4

The Rise of Nationalism and Communism

Overview

The authors provide an overview of the period subsequent to World War I, the interwar period, and the rise of conditions which contributed to the World War II experience. The rise of nationalism during this period took different forms in each of the countries discussed - the Philippines, Japan, Korea, and China - depending on their unique history, leadership, and national culture and the nature of their experience with European colonial powers.

The goals of democracy, progress and independence which emerged from the ideals of the Versailles Treaty (1919) were quickly and easily incorporated into the national aspirations of each of the Asian countries. Realizing national self-determination was more difficult. The counter forces arose from remaining colonial authorities and reflexive colonial mind sets as well as the reality of traditional societies based on class stratification and rural economies.

The Philippine fight for national self-determination against Spanish colonialism pitted the *peninsulares, creoles,* and *mestizos* against each other in a variety of programs ranging from conservative, nationalist to radial and revolutionary. The two best known leaders of this early Philippine Revolution (1896-1898) were Emilio Aguinaldo and Apolinario Mabini who did not work together resulting in prolonged and indeterminant violence. Neither were the *illustrados*, members of the constituent assembly, able to produce a common strategy or self-defense resulting in a takeover by the United States. U.S. colonialism replaced Spanish colonialism when Commodore George Dewey obliterated the Spanish squadron on May 1, 1898.

United States' foreign policy towards the Philippines was motivated by missionary zeal, social Darwinism, the Mahan's theory of sea power, and the lure of the Chinese market. This is encapsulated in a statement by the United States president, William McKinley, when he announced that he had no choice but "to educate the Filipinos and uplift and civilize and Christianize them, and by God's grace do the very best we could by them."

A change in United States' policy in 1990 reflected new thinking: colonialism should be self-liquidating and Filipinos should be taught and prepared for self-governance. Juan Sumulong pressed for gradual independence while the *nacionalistas* demanded immediate self-government. In 1916, the U.S. Congress under a democratic administration, passed the Jones Act promising independence as soon as a stable government could be established. A stable government was never established but the Hare-Hawes Cutting Bill granting independence was finally passed in 1941. Two common patterns emerged during the period between 1900 and 1941: (1) Economic class distinctions continued despite increasing education and urbanization, and (2) universal support for Philippine nationalism.

The Indonesian experience was both similar and different from that of the Philippines. The Sarekat Islam led by Tjokroaminoto and later Hatta, was split into nationalist and communist wings after repressive measures conducted by the Dutch authorities. The nationalists eventually prevailed under the leadership of Sukarno.

Two major events took place at Tian'anmen Square separated by almost sixty years of history: On May 4, 1919, several thousand students from Beijing's thirteen universities gathered in protest at the Gate of Heavenly Peace. This was the symbolic birth time of "modern" China in this century although it was actually part of the larger New Culture Movement which embraced a wide range of new ideas and artistic forms. It also expressed societal disillusionment over the failure of the Quin dynasty's reforms and the institution of a series of inept and corrupt warlords. Two major reformist factions were organized, one which was rather conservative advocating moderate forms and led by Liang Qichao. The other, was a radical faction led by Sun Yat-sen who had taken liberal democratic ideology to its logical conclusion in China. Revolution and change were inevitable and may have succeeded in installing a democratic regime in China were it not for the outbreak of World War I, the power of the Japanese military, and the power of a new ideology -- communism. The Chinese Communist Party (CCP) was allowed to participate in the democratic process and the reconstruction of the Nationalist Party (KMT). The party transformed Sun's 1905 platform, "Three Principles of the People" (nationalism, democracy and the people's livelihood), into a call for mass mobilization of peasants and workers. Marxism had a special appeal. It was both an ideology and a means of restoring a rightful order in the universe. Under the powerful leadership of Zhou Enlai, Deng Xiaoping and Mao Zedong, it captured the minds and hearts of the Chinese people. In 1927, the U.S. educated and trianed Chiang Kai-shek moved against the CCP. He eventually lost -- the battle with the Japanese in Manchuria and the battle for China to the Communists.

Vietnam had an equally traumatic experience. The early social--political movements reflected a combination of Confucianism, nationalism and liberal ideology. The threat of revolution was met by the French who subjected the Vietnamese leadership to harsh, repressive measurements. This led to more organized resistance. Ironically, this was led by the nearly 100,000 Vietnamese who had worked in Europe during the First World War and whose leadership had learned the benefits of democracy, capitalism and liberalism -- and wished those benefits for their own country. The well-traveled, well-educated and charismatic, Ho Chi Minh, formed the Indochina Communist Party and led the battle for independence. When Japan established effective control over the French in Vietnam, Ho's reaction was to organize guerrilla forces to fight first the Japanese, and then the French.

On March 3, 1919, a group of Korean patriots read aloud a Declaration of

Independence that stated that the Koreans were a free, united people with 5,000 years of history. Although immediately arrested by the Japanese police, this became the symbol of Korea's initial movement to democracy. American educated, Dr. Philip Jaisohn, formed the Independence Club and supported freedom, independence nationalism, and capitalism. This New Korean Enlightenment was not favored by the powerful Japanese. Resistance led to repression, and repression led to a split in the independence movement. Some of the leaders supported a moderate form of Korean democracy, others a more radical form. The "winner" was Syngman Rhee, a Christian, western-educated, heroic, relative of the former monarch, who became President in exile. The Korean communists were repressed by the Japanese which made them heroes. Led by the future dictator, Kim Il Sung, they were friendly with both the Chinese and Russians when it was in their best interest to do so

Outline

I. The Philippines
    A. Early nationalism
    B. Pre-World War II
II. Indonesia
    A. Uniqueness of Indonesian experience
    B. Social change and nationalism
III. China
    A. 1919 and the May Fourth Movement
    B. The Late Qing Reforms
    C. Revolution of 1911
        1. Sun Yat-Sen
        2. Liang Qichao
    D. Asian Power and China on the eve of World War I
    E. The appeal of Marxism-Leninism in China and the rest of Asia
        1. Early communism
        2. Chaing Kai-shek
        3. Zhou Enlai
        4. Mao Zedong
    F. New Culture movement
        1. Individualism, iconoclasm and other isms
        2. Hu Shi and the colloquial literature movement
        3. Split in the movement
        4. Lu Xun
    G. A golden age of Chinese capitalism (1911-1937)
IV. Vietnam
    A. Early nationalism
    B. Emergence of organized resistance
    C. Ho Chi Minh and the Indochina Communist Party
V. Korea
    A. 1919 and the March First Movement
    B. The Independence Club
    C. The New Korean Enlightenment

　　　　　　1.　　Resistance Movements
　　　　　　2.　　Increasing industrialism
　　　　　　3.　　Korean communists
VI.　　Japan
　　　A.　　Response to the Versailles Conference
　　　B.　　Economic turmoil and aftermath of the war boom
　　　C.　　Influence of the military between 1918 and 1930
　　　D.　　Democracy and the role of the Emperor
　　　E.　　The national mood
　　　F.　　National debate and the trial of Minobe
　　　G.　　Kita Ikki and Japan's Angry Young Men
　　　H.　　The Sino-Japanese War (1937)

THE PHILIPPINES

Terms	Names:	Dates
peninsulares	Jose Rizal	1986-1989
creoles mestizos	Emilio Aguinaldo	Philippine
ilustrados	Commondore	Revolution
Tagalog	George Dewey	1898
mestizos	Apolinario Mabini	Commodore
ilustrados	Captain Alfred	Dewey
Tagalog	Thayer Mahan	1919
Katipunan	President William	Treaty of
self-liquidating	McKinley	Versailles
imperialism	Jacob Schurman	1916 the Jones Act
land tenure	Juan Sumulong	1941 Hare-Hawes-
Wood-Forbes	Leonard Wood/	Cutting
mission	William C. Forbes	
	Sergio Osmena	
	Manual Quezo	

INDONESIA

Terms	Names	Dates
Ethical Policy of the Dutch	Tjokroaminoto	1942
Sarekat Islam	Sukarno	
Indonesian Nationalist Party (PNI)	Hatta	
National Education Club		
Java		
Guided Democracy		

CHINA

Terms	Names	Dates
May Fourth Movement	Qing Empress Dowager Cixi	May 4, 1919
New Culture Movement	Sun Yat-Sen	
Gates of Heavenly Peace	Liang Qichao	
Three Principles of the People	Chaing Kai-shek	
CCP	Zhou Enlai	
Guomindang	Deng Xiaoping	
Manchukuo	Mao Zedong	
the Long March	Hu Shi	
intelligentsia	Lu Xun	

VIETNAM
Dong Du Movement
Ho Chi Minh
Hue
Phan Chu trinh
Viet Minh

JAPAN
February 26th Incident
Inukai Tsuyoshi
Taisho Emperor (Yoshihito)
Chrysanthemum Throne

KOREA
The Independence Club
Dr. Philip Jaisohn

Key Concepts

<u>yellow peril</u>: a popular term that referred to the perceived menace that the Chinese and Japanese presented to the West, both in Asia and at home

Western learning (sohak): first used to refer to Roman Catholicism and later to Western science

Manifest Destiny: the doctrine that God had given a special inheritance to the country associated and had both the right and duty to take enlightenment to foreign regions. Used to support territorial and cultural imperialism.

receptivity: term used to refer to the degree of cultural openness to new ideas and technologies

legitimacy: the degree to which a government reflects the needs and wishes of its citizenry. It is assumed that democracy is the most legitimate of governmental forms.

business conglomerates (zaibatsu): cooperation and networking between various businesses and government

anachronism: something out of place or unsuited to its time

undeclared war: hostilities between political units without governmental prior notification. Recommended in the teachings of Sun Tsu.

idealists: visionary or one whose conduct is influenced by a set of ideals held in relationship to perfection

extremists: those individuals who take out of the ordinary measures to support a particular belief system or ideology

Knowledge, understanding and evaluation

1. Understand that the division between nationalism and communism in this period was a result of differing ideologies, leadership, experience and vision.

2. The leaders of the emerging states of Asia had confidence in the value of education.

3. The vision of the Versailles Treaty can not be overstated in its influence on Asian thinking.

4. Class divisions became more important and more apparent in this era as a result of the development of communication technology.

5. This period was especially important in the changing nature of civil-military relationships. The military as supportive of order in society was set in opposition to the disorderly nature of emerging democracy.

6. Charismatic leadership was especially significant in focusing the economic and political development of specific countries.

7. The Sino-Japanese War of 1937 signaled a new era in military confrontation and the emerging power of Japan.

8. Secret societies and criminal organizations increased in direct relationship to governmental repression whether indigenous or colonial.

9. There are significant inter-relationships between and among government, business, banking, the military and elites of Asia which make them seem impenetrable to outsiders.

10. This was a period of rapid economic growth for the economies of Asian countries.

Topics for Research Papers

The Writings of Sun Yat-Sen
Chiang Kai Shek: Hero or Villain?
Ho Chi Minh as a Leader
The Influence of French Education on the Development of Revolution in Asia
John Dewey's Influence on Asian Education
The Comintern and the Development of Asian Communism
The City of Shanghai

The Long March
The Women's Movement in China
Catholicism in Vietnam
Philip Jaisohn and the Independence Club
Revolutionary Music in China, Vietnam and Japan
The Mukden Incident of 1931
Syngman Rhee, a Christian Korean
The *Zaibatsu* and the Militarization of Japan

CHAPTER 5

Maelstrom: The Pacific War and its Aftermath

Overview

This chapter describes one of the most <u>important eras of change in Pacific history.</u> The beginning of the era in the late 1930's until the period of the Bandung Conference in 1955 the period is characterized by war, revolution, and violence. The deployment of the atomic bomb changed the very nature of world politics. It not only demonstrated the horrifying nature of the weapon but illustrated the relationship between technological superiority and political hegemony.

By the 1930's, <u>Japan</u> had demonstrated that she was a world power - economically and militarily. The rationalizations given for imperialism were standard world power justifications: ridding the region of outsiders, liberating captive populations, and installing a better, more efficient form of government.

The <u>United States</u> came into confrontation with Japan motivated by the China connection, the existence of natural resources in the area, as a consequence of "great-power" competition, viewing the Japanese state as of the same ilk as Nazi Germany and finally, the bombing of Pearl Harbor on 7 December 1942. The United States won the war after unrelenting firebombing of Japan and the use of the atomic bomb on Hiroshima 6 August 1945.

General Douglas MacArthur was in charge of the occupation of Japan. A number of important changes were made in response to the perceived requirement to demilitarize Japan and make her incapable of waging war any time in the future. (Note the discussion of Article 9) Under a very pragmatic and seemingly expansive regime, the emperor was reduced to symbol of the nation, education was extended, land reform managed and a new constitution adopted. Whether the culture of interdependence (relation ships between business, government and elites) was changed significantly remains a subject of dispute. Occupation finally ended with the Treaty of San Francisco in 1952.

The Indonesian experience was difficult and rather bloody. The Dutch were supplanted by the Japanese in August of 1945 and their return prevented by a bloody civil war. The new country of Indonesia was established through the auspices of the United Nations, world opinion and as a consequence of war weariness. Sukarno who had fought long and hard for independence became Indonesia's first president.

The Philippine experience was equally troubling. The Hukbalahap were unable to mount final effective resistance against the Japanese and, in part, blamed this on lack of adequate support from the United States. Independence was finally achieved when guerrilla leader, Ramon Magsaysay saved the day. He later was responsible for arresting the Communist Party Politburo, establishing a fledgling democracy and becoming its first president. The U.S. retained Subic Bay and Clark Air Field.

Vietnam was another story. In spite of the activities of the Viet Minh liberation army and the brilliant leadership of Giap and Ho Chi Minh, the Japanese destroyed French Indo-China destroyed in less than 24 hours. The occupation lasted from 1941 to 1945. Ho remains a controversial figure in world politics. He was by all accounts, pro democratic, nationalist and a good military strategists. (On one occasion, he is given credit for organizing the resistance to a Chinese invasion army of 180,000 men.) The French colonialists were reluctant to leave Vietnam and after a bitter, protracted and bloody attempt to remain in control, finally left under the agreements reached in Geneva in 1954. Vietnam was partitioned and the problems remained unresolved until hostilities were renewed with American intervention in the 1960's.

One of the more interesting diplomatic conferences ever held was the <u>Bandung Conference of 1955</u>. It was a seminal event which changed the political and organizational temper of the region. Zhou Enlai, China's spokesman, was an effective representative reminding the world of the existence of the large neighbor to the north. He basically supported the independence of Laos, Vietnam and Cambodia while condemning U.S. presence in the region by attacking SEATO indirectly. He avoided direct confrontation over Taiwan in a skillful use of diplomacy. Japan remained a somewhat passive participant given its recent history and worked behind the scenes to press her own interests.

Outline

I. Japan and the United States at war
    Seizure of Manchuria
        A.   Japan's rationalizations
            1.   "Great power" status and rights
            2.   Liberation of southeast Asia
        B.   U.S. interests
            1.   China connection
            2.   Natural resources
            3.   Power confrontation
            4.   Japanese state as Nazi-like
            5.   Pearl Harbor and Pacific fleet
        C.   The War in the Pacific
            1.   Firebombing
            2.   End with bombing of Hiroshima on 6 August 1945
        D.   U.S. and Japan immediately after the war
            1.   U.S. policy of occupation
                  a.   Emperor as symbol
                  b.   General MacArthur's pragmatism
            2.   Changes
                  a.   Economic organization remained

                b.   Education
                c.   De-militarization
                d.   Constitution
                e.   Land reform
        3.   Article Nine
        4.   1952 Treaty of San Francisco

I. Indonesia
    A.   Japanese colonial rule ends in August 1945
    B.   Dutch colonial rule challenged with bloody civil war
    C.   Institution of the state of "Indonesia"
        1.   U.N. intervention, 1948
        2.   The *pemuda* movement
        3.   Sukarno becomes President

II. The Philippines
    A.   Japanese rule
        1.   Contested by the Hukbalahap
        2.   U.S. seen as non-supportive
    B.   Independence
        1.   Ramon Magsaysay: guerrilla leader to president
        2.   Arrest of Communist Party Politburo
    C.   U.S. Retention of Subic Bay and Clark Air Field

III. Vietnam
    A.   French Indo-China destroyed in less than 24 hours
    B.   Japanese occupation from 1941 to 1945
    C.   The Viet Minh liberation army
    D.   Ho Chi Minh
        1.   Pro-democratic
        2.   Repels Chinese invasion army of 180,000 men
        3.   Relationship with the French and renewal of fighting
        4.   Geneva Agreement of 1954
                a.   French withdrawal
                b.   Partition of Vietnam

IV. Bandung conference
    A.   Built on Geneva Agreements of 1954
    B.   Zhou Enlai becomes spokesman
        1.   Supports independence of Laos, Vietnam and

45

               Cambodia
      2.   Condemns SEATO
      3.   Avoids confrontation over Taiwan
      4.   Skillful use of diplomacy
  C.   Japanese passive participant

Key Terms

Axis and Allied Powers
Greater East Asia Co-Prosperity Sphere
San Francisco Peace Treaty
Viet Minh
Hukbalahap resistance
Bandung Conference

Names	Places	Dates
Gen. Douglas MacArthur	Nagasaki	7 December 1941
Sukarno	Hiroshima	6 August 1945
Ramon Magsaysay	Manchuria	2 September 1945
Ferdinand Marcos	French Indo-China	1952 San Francisco Peace Treaty
Vo Nguyen Giap	Subic Bay	
Ho Chi Minh	Clark Air Field	
Zhou Enlai	Hanoi	

Key Concepts

<u>Allies:</u> China, France, the United Kingdom, the United States, and the U.S.S.R. now permanent members of the U.N. Security Council.

<u>Axis:</u> the vanquished countries of the Tripartite Pact of World War I including Germany, Italy and Japan.

46

ethnocentrism: the belief that one's ethnic or cultural group is superior to others. Race and culture are central considerations.

militarism: glorification of the military and its predominance in the policy and administration of a state.

Fascism: system of government based on the authority or dictatorship of the extreme right.

Article 9: section of the postwar "peace" Constitution of Japan which renounces war as a sovereign right of the national and the use of force of settling international disputes. Prohibits the building of an offensive military capability.

collective security: a system of world order in which aggression by any state would be met by a collective response.

limited war; war of attribution: hostilities which are not "all out war" wherein the goal is to wear on the patience and perserverance of the enemy rather than defeat it on the field of battle.

incendiary raid: the use of bombs to produce fires; overall killed more people and destroyed more property that the atomic bomb in Japan.

atomic bomb: explosive weapon wherein destructive power is derived from the rapid release of energy in the fission of heavy atomic nuclei. Used at Hiroshima and Nagasaki in 1945.

Knowledge, understanding, evaluation

1. It is critical to understand Japan's understanding of the meaning of "world power."

2. The relationship between Japan and other Asian countries continues to reflect Japanese occupation during the Second World War.

3. The United States believes it behaved as a good occupation force and should be appreciated by the Japanese people. The Japanese perspective is much different.

4. There is an important controversy about whether the Japanese culture is "suitable" for democracy given the cultural and economic inter-relationships such as the *zaibatsu*.

5. The Philippine people believe that the United States has not treated them fairly and has behaved in a colonial and imperious manner. This will effect future foreign policy in the region and contributed to the closure of Subic Bay and Clark Air Field.

6. There were many short term and long term effects of the atomic bombing of Hiroshima and Nagasaki. One school of thought in Japan is that the United States won because of technological, nor moral or political, superiority.

7. A combination of the end of colonialism and Japanese occupation worked to destabilize the entire region for a number of years. This was unsettling both to the inhabitants and meant that U.S. foreign policy was less than consistent. The specter of communism was probably exaggerated in this unsettled atmosphere. This would have especially important consequences for Indonesia, Malaysia and Vietnam.

8. Communism and nationalism may be separate ideologies but both were often indistinguishable at this time.

9. Ho Chi Minh was an important and gifted leader of his people.

10. China's interests were effectively presented by Zhou Enlai at the Bangdung Conference in 1955. He would remain and important personage in Chinese foreign policy and Asian politics until his death in the middle 1990s.

Topics for Research Papers

1. Hiroshima
2. The Firebombing of Tokyo
3. The Reemergence of the Greater East Asia Co-Prosperity Sphere
4. The Story of General Douglas MacArthur
5. The Constitution of Japan
6. Article Nine of the Constitution of Japan and the Problem of U.N. Peacekeeping
7. Pearl Harbor
8. De-Militarization of Japan 1945 to 1952
9. The Education of Giap
10. The Story of Ho Chi Minh

CHAPTER 6

Miracle by Design: The Postwar Resurgence of Japan

Overview

Japan came out of the war experience with some important assets: a returned population that provided a surplus labor, an educated population, an outward looking international vision, and a collective experience of how to build and operate an industrial economy. It moved from being defeated, dependent and developing nation to an economic dynamo. Japan is now in a new period of adjustment looking for a new vision and visionary leadership.

The American occupiers in cooperation with Japanese industrial leadership mandated the closure of state financial institutions and corporations, demilitarization of industry, breakup of the *zaibatsu*, the reorganization of the land system, suppression of the labor movement, and a new form of democratic governance. The U.S. government originally exacted reparation payments, then established a Reconstruction Finance Bank, and later end that support as recommended by Joseph Dodge. After a period of turmoil, an economic boom resulted from Korean War (1950) purchases by the U.S. government. An important decision was made: not to spend national resources on national defense but to rely on the U.S. "umbrella."

New bargains were struck with the Japanese people. The prospect of lifetime employment took the place of union organization. There was an emphasis on heavy industry and the promise of economic growth. Where Japan did very well between 1950 and 1980, the Japanese people did not reap immediate benefits. Consumer goods were scarce, land prices high, rice was subsidized but expensive, and the government manipulated the currency to encourage savings and investment by private citizens. The oil crisis of 1973 precipitated a downturn in the Japanese economy and also encouraged investment in natural gas and other critical energy sources.

Managed trade and seemingly unfair trade practices became a problem in the international economy. The United States and European Union, in particular, pressured Japan to enact reforms that would (1) direct capital surpluses towards public investment in Japan to improve the quality of life and at the same time stimulate demand for foreign goods and services, (2) change land policy prices, (3) revises rules to permit easier entry by foreign retailers, (4) control the *keiretsu*, and (5) make the system more transparent. By 1990 these measures had been attempted but serious recession moderated the effects.

The Greater East Asia Co-prosperity Sphere and World War II activities had lasting effect on Japan's diplomatic and economic relationships in the region. Japan took a cautious approach with neighbors and for some time relied extensively on the United States' market. It has more recently moved towards both Europe and South Asia. One of Japan's major concerns is ensuring a constant and predictable supply of energy at a low price. Maintenance of good relationships with various Middle East petroleum producing countries (including Saudi Arabia and the other Gulf States) Iran, and Iraq are considered critical national security concerns.

The deeply held Japanese faith in government bureaucratic management of industry was shaken by the country's economic troubles in the 1990s. The rest of the world had to reassess the "Japanese miracle." Chalmers Johnson categorizes four competing explanations: (1) no miracle occurred, (2) national character, basic values and consensus, (3) unique structural features, and (4) the free rider status in relationship to the United States. The Japanese economic organization has been unique in form and organization which allowed it great initial success but is also responsible for the unique problems which result from that same organization.

It is not possible to understand the economic system without understanding its relationship to the political system. To a greater degree than in most countries, they work in tangent. The Liberal Democratic Party (LDP) originally formed as a coalition of political factions, ruled without interruption from 1955 to 1993. Its fall came as a result of domestic dissatisfaction, internal party fractures, and international pressures and was precipitated by economic recession.

There is some dispute as to whether Japanese political culture will elicit strong leadership by a single individual or party, or whether government by elite consensus will remain the dominant political form.

Another interesting issue is whether the Japanese public with access to more information as a result of communication and technological advances, will demand a more democratic and responsive government. It also remains to be seen how and to what degree resurgent nationalism will effect Japan's domestic and international agendas.

Outline

I. After World War II
    A. Assets: returned population, educated, outward looking and collective experience.
    B. Liabilities: defeated, dependent, developing and making significant changes

II. The American occupiers
    A. Early programs
        1. Mandated the closure of state financial institutions and corporations
        2. Demilitarization of industry
        3. Breakup of the *zaibatsu*
        4. Reorganization of the land system
        5. Suppression of the labor movement
        6. New form of democratic governance
    B. U.S. financial initiatives
        1. Reparation payments
        2. Reconstruction Finance Bank

            3. Joseph Dodge recommends termination of Bank
        C. Turn-around
            1. Korean War (1950) purchases by the U.S. government
            2. Decision not to spend national resources on national defense but to rely on the U.S. "umbrella"
III. Domestic arrangements
    A. Promise of lifetime employment took the place of union organization
    B. Emphasis on heavy industry and the promise of economic growth
    C. 1950 to 1980, the Japanese people did not reap benefits in proportion to growth
        1. Consumer goods scarce
        2. Land prices high
        3. Rice was subsidized but expensive
        4. Government encouragement for savings and investment
        5. The oil crisis of 1973 encouraged investment in natural gas and other critical energy sources
IV. International problems
    A. Managed trade and seemingly unfair trade practices became a problem
    B. Pressured to enact reforms that would
        1. Direct capital surpluses towards public investment in Japan to improve the quality of life and at the same time stimulate demand for foreign goods and services
        2. Change land policy prices
        3. Permit easier entry by foreign retailers
        4. Control the *keiretsu*
        5. Make the system more transparent
    C. By 1990 measures had been attempted but serious recession moderated the effects.
V. Four ways of reassessing the "Japanese miracle"
    A. No miracle occurred
    B. National character, basic values, and consensus,

        C. Unique structural features
        D. Free rider status in relationship to the United States.
VI. The political system and the economy
        A. Rule by the Liberal Democratic Party (LDP) ends in 1993
        B. Fall a result of domestic dissatisfaction, internal party fractures, and international pressures
        C. Precipitated by economic recession
        D. Dispute as to whether Japanese political culture will elicit strong leadership by a single individual or party, or whether government by elite consensus will remain the dominant political form
        E. Japanese public may demand more democratic and responsive
        F. Problem of national pride versus resurgent nationalism
VII. Contemporary place in world economy and international affairs

Terms
keiretsu
MITI
free rider
Nissan Strike
Kawasaki Steel
Dodge Mission
Reconstruction Finance Bank
Korean War boom
Japanese Miracle

Names
Chalmers Johnson

Dates
1985 Plaza Accord
1993 defeat of LDP

Key Concepts

"beggar thy neighbor" trade policy: efforts to promote domestic welfare by promoting trade surpluses that can be realized only at other countries' expense.

information society: an inter-related world economy based on modern technology such as computers, facsimiles and shared data bases. The emphasis is on intangibles, not physical products and facilities.

Multinational Corporation (MNC): a company which operates in several countries such as Shell, Norelco, Guinnes, Honda, IBM, Mitsubishi, Sony, and Nissan.

market rational\ plan rational: both terms refer to economic systems. A market rational economy reflects any changes in the basic market forces (i.e., supply and demand) and has limited governmental regulation. A plan rational economy reflects the formulation and implementation of an economic policy and close cooperation between business and government.

oil crisis: The two major oil crises were in 1973-74 and 1979-80 when OPEN used oil supplies as a political weapon against industrialized countries.

lifetime employment: a system which treat employees as human capital and a resource to be developed rather than as a simple business expense. There is an emphasis on retraining, loyalty and company ethic and is generally supported only by large and profitable corporations.

applied and basic research: Applied research finds practical applications for the findings of basic research. It is hence more immediately profitable to business and industry.

heavy industry: industry such as electric power, coal, shipping and steel production which contribute to the infra structural development of a country.

transparency: in economic or political systems, this term refers to the degree of openness to outsiders. It is a requisite of democracy but not necessarily of capitalism; transparency is extremely difficult to achieve in organizations which combine government and industry.

company union/ industry union: unions whose membership is based in either one company or across an entire industry. Company unions are more easily manipulated or broken not having the resources to balance company power.

free rider: those who enjoy the benefits of collective goods but pay little or nothing for them.

Knowledge, understanding, and evaluation

1. One of the most important points in this chapter is that the Japanese economy has not been an unqualified success. There have been significant problems for the Japanese people, the region and the world economy.

2. The *keiretsu* system should be compared to the *zaibatsu* system with regard to assumptions of mutual obligation.

3. The trade-off between a promise of lifetime employment and lack of union representation was clearly more favorable to industry than to individual workers. It is important to understand that this elite management is consistent with managed economies and the rule of the LDP. It may be benevolent in intent as well as restrictive of individual freedoms.

4. The short term effects of the Dodge Mission were associated with a painful readjustment of the Japanese economy; the long term effects may have been to undercut Japanese trust of U.S. intentions.

5. There is significant disagreement about the relationship between the low level of defense expenditures and the growth of the Japanese economy. Please take note that 1 percent of the G.D.P. in Japan represents quite a large sum of money.

6. Another disagreement is whether the events at Nagasaki and Hiroshima have produced a pacifist population or whether militarism is alive and well.

7. The Diet is Japan's legislative body. Election rules and regulations regarding individual member's association with *keritsu* are a constant source of dispute.

8. The failure of the LDP in 1993 surprised the party as well as the public. However, it may have both reflected and produced a new level of public participation in government.

9. The Ministry of Trade and Industry (MITI) has been an important factor in the managed control of the economy.

10. Japan's economic record has some major blemishes:

- With regard to research and development, Japan lags seriously.

- It contributes less to global scientific knowledge than expected.

- Average Japanese productivity levels remain well below those of the U.S. and Germany.

- In critical areas of retailing and telecommunications, it is behind.

- The policy environment continues to stall growth.

- Environmental policy, especially with regard to Japanese industry in the region) is virtually nonexistent.

- Agricultural policy as noted by the extraordinarily high price of rice is clearly a result of subjective rather than economic factors.

- The financial market is fragile.

- Land speculation is a continuing problem.

- There is a major problem with the lack of sustained vision on the part of political and economic leadership.

Topics for Research Papers

1. MITI
2. The Dodge Mission
3. The Fall of the Liberal Democratic Party
4. The Effects of Low Spending on Defense

5. Did Hiroshima Produce a Pacifist Japan?
6. The European Union and Japan
7. Japan's Trading Problems with France
8. Leadership Before and After World War II
9. Japan's New Nationalism
10. The Portrayal of World War II in Japanese Elementary School Textbooks

CHAPTER 7

The New Asian Capitalists

Overview

The strategic control or domination of markets, with the support of government, is the major priority in the Asian model of capitalism. The alternative strategy, that espoused by the United States and Europe, is of "free trade," i.e., markets and market pricing allowed to develop without being manipulated by government and companies. This competing visions of capitalism are a source of considerable tension and misunderstanding.

As was discussed in the previous chapter, Japan has led the region and is the premier developed economic. In 1960 it accounted for approximately 20 percent of the region's income and 3 percent of that of the world. In 1975 these figures stood at approximately 50 percent and 9 percent, respectively. The growth rate has levelled but the share is still of great significance.

The authors organize other growth regions as those of (1) South Korea, Taiwan, Hong Kong and Singapore, (2) resource-rich countries in Southeast Asia including Malaysia, Thailand, Indonesia, and the Philippines; and (3) the People's Republic of China.

The Newly Industrializing Countries (NIEs) are the high growth economies of

East Asia (South Korea, Taiwan, Hong Kong and Singapore) and have shared several characteristics. (1) The governments participated in strategic planning and cooperated with the private sector to promote specific national industries; (2) All shared a commitment to export-oriented growth; and (3) All had high levels of savings and investment often exceeding 20 percent or more of GNP which is widely held to be a level at which development becomes self-sustaining.

These countries entered the world economic environment at a time in which there were favorable conditions. Each had a significant prewar experience with nascent industrialization that they were able to build on. It usually believed that the governments in the region were unusually important factors in the post war period both politically and economically and were able to leverage this power in the development of national economic strategies. The political consensus on economic development as an overriding national objective justified a strong governmental role in charting and guiding economic growth. Whatever remained of the power of a wealthy landowning class had been minimized as a consequence of the war so that force for conservative policies was absent. The working class and associated labor movements were so impacted by the war that it was not able to organize, mobilize, or effectively articulate their interests. Political stability, whether repressive or simply conservative, pertained in each of the countries which enhanced the possibility of government focus on economic matters.

The economic strategies went from import substitution during the 1950s to the mid 1960s, export oriented industrialization from the 1960s to the 1970s and then more advanced export strategies in the 1980s. Sector development also proceeded similarly in each of these countries. Agricultural production which is labor intensive, was encouraged but prices kept at a level which would generate national income which could be then used to support textiles and other light industry development. Income generated from that sector was then used for investment in heavy industry. Heavy industry was eventually supplanted by high technology industry which represents a high capital investment strategies which generate larger profit margins. The authors note that as late as 1960 agricultural products accounted for 37 percent of South Korea's gross domestic product compared to the 1990s wherein industrial production accounts for 90 percent of

Korea's gross domestic product.

Cultural values also supported economic development. The Confucian values of hard work, savings, discipline, secularism, entrepreneurship and educational attainment do not automatically lead to economic development (as noted by the fact that other countries with Confucian values are NOT economically successful) but it is certain that these values support an orientation that is conductive to the formulation of policies at the public and private levels.

The members of ASEAN (the Association of Southeast Asian Nations) are Brunei, Burma, Indonesia, Laos, Malaysia, the Philippines, Singapore, Thailand and Vietnam. Brunei is a singular case -- an oil-rich sultanate with a per capital income of over US $20,000. Singapore is a newly rich financial center. Indonesia, Malaysia, the Philippines and Thailand are middle-income countries comparatively rich in primary products. These economies have had recently high rates of growth and have undergone significant structural transformation.

Outline

I. Commonalities in successful economic growth
    A. Government participation and cooperation with private sector
    B. Commitment to export-oriented growth
    C. High levels of saving

II. Japan
    A. Now 50 percent of region's income and 9 percent of world's income
    B. Growth rate dropping

III. Newly Industrializing Economies of Hong Kong, Singapore, South Korea, and Taiwan
    A. Understanding success
        1. Favorable world economic environment
        2. Start during the prewar period
        3. Strong governmental role
        4. Absence of wealthy landowning class

			5.	Weak labor movement
			6.	Strong economic bureaucracies
			7.	Political stability
		B.	Strategies
			1.	Import substitution (1950s to mid 1960s)
			2.	Export oriented industrialization (1960s -- 1970s)
			3.	Advanced Export strategies (1980s)
		C.	Sector development
			1.	Agriculture
			2.	Textiles
			3.	Light industry
			4.	Heavy industry
			5.	High technology
IV.	ASEAN: Brunei, Burma, Indonesia, Laos, Malaysia, the Philippines, Singapore, Thailand, Vietnam
		A.	ASEAN-4: Indonesia, Malaysia, the Philippines, Thailand
		B.	Low income economies: Burma, Vietnam, Kampuchea, Laos
V.	Symbolism of rice and land distribution
VI.	Korea: the "Miracle on the Han" as an example of Asian economic development
		A.	Japanese influence
			1.	Impact of Japanese colonialism as foundation for economic transformation
			2.	Post-war influence
		B.	U.S. war and post-war contributions
			1.	Source of capital
			2.	No military expenditure
			3.	Education
			4.	Technology transfers
		C.	Record from 1963 to 1990
			1.	Vietnam War economy
			2.	ROK--Japan Normalization Treaty of 1965
		D.	Internal factors
			1.	Lack of landed elite
			2.	Dynamic entrepreneurs
			3.	Labor

    4. Injection of foreign capital
    5. Openness to technology
    6. Entrepreneurial growth
  E. Role of government
    1. Government of Park Chung Hee
    2. Five-year development plans
    3. State controls and incentives
    4. Flexibility in relationship to business and labor
  F. Role of culture
    1. National identity and pride
    2. Confucian tradition and a tendency toward individual self-assertion
    3. New Calvinism and Christian influences
  G. Importance of timing
    1. War economies
    2. International economic growth period
    3. Mentorship of Japan
  H. Problems
    1. Distribution of wealth
    2. Too much state control may require privatization
    3. Reliance on foreign capital
    4. Political volatility
    5. Confucian and traditional commitment to harmonious relationships and mutual obligation
VII. Confucian traditions in Asian economies
  A. Small family business and large corporations
  B. Education
  C. Management and the moral environment
  D. Confucianism with a capitalist face"
VIII. Overseas ethnic Chinese
  A. Historical factors and maintenance of family ties
  B. Colonial separation
  C. Marriage at a distance
  D. Adaptation to vagaries of international commerce

Key Terms

import substitution
export led growth
labor intensive
protectionism
Newly Industrialized Economies (NIEs)
ASEAN
ASEAN-4
"Miracle on the Han"
"Confucianism with a capitalist face"

Key Concepts

<u>bureaucratic capitalism</u>: term used specifically with reference to the Republican Era in China (1928-1945). The term reflects both the traditional importance of the civil servant in society and the newly recognized power associated with the accumulation of wealth through capital investment. In Republican China, four wealthy extended families maintained dominance in both politics and economics and utilized that dominance to influence both the domestic and international policies of their country.

<u>overseas Chinese</u>: The dispersed Chinese emigre community that maintains cultural loyalty and political interest in modern China.

<u>Gross Domestic Product</u> (GDP): the revenue from production only and not to revenue from services or from extra-national sources.

<u>New Industrialized Economy</u> (NIE): States industrialized only within this century including Hong Kong, South Korea, Singapore, and Taiwan.

<u>import substitution</u>: the promotion of domestic manufacture through special import tariffs, or through subsidies to domestic industries, or a combination of the two.

meritocracy: A term used to refer to a situation wherein bureaucratic advancement based on earned (ability) rather than ascribed characteristics (race, gender, wealth, etc). Meritocracies are often characterized by a professional civil service wherein advancement in based on individual achievement.

industrial-commercial corporations (chaebol): economic interests and investments across many sectors. Chaebol are the Korean equivalent of Japanese Keiretsu (prewar, zaibatsu)

labor intensive: those industries which have high input of human labor as opposed to capital or technology intensive industries. Most often associated with agriculture, art and handicrafts.

technology transfer: the movement of technology both in the form of ideas and actual machinery from a technologically rich environment to one which is in need of a particular technology for economic production and development.

terms of trade: the ratio of export prices to import prices. Many developing countries maintain that the prices they receive for their exports fall in the long run while the prices of the manufactured goods they import increase steadily creating a negative trade balance.

entrepreneurial: a person who organizes, operates, and assumes the risk associated with business ventures.

Knowledge, understanding and evaluation

1. There is a tendency to over-generalize about Asian economies. The authors of this chapter make a point of describing similarities as well as differences for each of the countries in the region.

2. The Japanese "model" can not be taken as a whole or static design for economic development as each of the countries has a different set of resources and resource constraints.

3. Whatever the reasons, economic growth and development in the region between the end of World War II and the present time has been truly remarkable. Perhaps as a direct result, many of the other political, social, and environmental problems are either overlooked or overshadowed. (This is no different in some respects than the over-simplified view of Africa as being a region of tribal conflict and environmental problems or of South America as being a product of dependency relationships.) A balanced and wholeistic view of Asia is supported by the authors of this text.

4. East Asian managerial practices take personal values seriously and strive to create a corporate culture different from the formalistic, contractual ideals of Western rational bureaucracies.

5. There are a number of countries in Asia that are NOT wealthy and have serious problems with their economies and that these problems may be more related to very difficult political systems than to natural resource endowments.

6. Korea was uniquely advantaged by its relationship with Japan and the United States. This was a country that combined resources and capabilities, and whose timing was right, to produce a high rate of economic growth.

7. Reunification of Korea is likely to have both economic and social costs which may change the rate of economic development.

8. The government of Korea may have to initiate programs designed to redistribute wealth and income.

9. Neo-Confucianism and capitalism may or may not be basically antagonistic but the relationship can be rationalized and behaviors adapted as required by modern civilization.

10. Overseas ethnic Chinese tend to maintain linkages with other Chinese families. This may have important consequences for being discriminated against in some of the countries of the region, in tracing international commercial linkages, and even finding criminal connections.

11. The aggregate economic growth of the Asian Pacific countries in the past three decades is unsurpassed by any other world region.

12. Asian industrialists and social elites tend to believe that stability is a critical factor supporting economic growth and development and that this can best be achieved by centrist or conservative governments.

13. United States' security interests in the region include economic, political, and military factors. All of these can be studied separately but are, in fact, interrelated. Reunification of Korea, for example, will affect economic relationships, political and diplomatic relationships and mandate a change in U.S. security policy in the region.

14. ASEAN is a regional, intergovernmental organization with its own dynamics. It is not comparable to the European Union which is a supragovernmental organization.

15. The United States, European, and Japanese stock markets and economic interdependencies will be increasingly important in the future. Problems in one of these major areas will necessarily affect all of the world's economic stability.

Topics for Research Papers

1. ASEAN and the EU: Differences and Similarities
2. The Changing Economy of Hong Kong
3. The Economic Development of Taiwan
4. Nike and the Labor Issue
5. The Price of Rice
6. The Effect of Population Growth on Asian Economies
7. Equity and Redistribution in the NIEs
8. Mitsubishi - from the Zero to U.S. Highways
9. Effects of the ROK-Japan Normalization Treaty
10. Women's Role in Asian Economic Development

CHAPTER 8

Power, Authority, and the Advent of Democracy

Overview

Each of the countries described in this chapter is unique. Each has a different combination of national resources, population profiles, colonial experience and set of problems with governmental transitions. The authors use the themes of power and authority to address the post World War II experiences of these countries.

Thailand experience has been of one military coup after another but this may not directly correlate with repressive practices. The military leadership believes in the principle of benevolent superiority i.e., that superior should behavior appropriately with others. This forms a philosophical bases for self control or internal control of military organizations. The problem stems from the preclusion of corrective mechanism i.e., there is no effective way to counter corruption, abuse and personal power when the government is under the control of people with guns.

Malaysia's population is divided between the ethnic Malay (45%), ethnic Chinese (35%) and Indians (10%). The professional and commercial sectors have traditionally been in the hands of the Chinese in a traditionally Malay country. In 1957, the delicately balanced multiethnic coalition led by Tanku

Abdul Rahman, was systematically undercut by ethnic and personal politics. Public riots on May 13, 1969 led to a reorganization of government which was nominally democratic but *defacto* in the hands of the Malay majority elites. By 1981, Dr. Mahathir Mohamad, was in control of this fragile state.

Indonesia is a large country with similar problems of ethnic diversity, political repression, lack of effective state control over border areas, and a difficult colonial heritage. Indonesia, however, has enormous natural resources and its own unique political history. This may be symbolized by the leadership of two men: Sukarno and Suharto. This transition between the regimes was characterized by extreme mass violence and state repression. Sukarno was intensely nationalistic. His regime, under the principles of "Guided Democracy" relied on the ethnical practice of *musyawarhar* (deliberation and consensus) and on the army whenever people were not properly "guided." The insurgency of 1965 was probably a result of a combination of economic problems, military adventurism, and corruption but was fiercely blamed on the Communist party (PCI) and minority ethnic fellow-travellers. What came out of the brutality was a New Order led by Sukarno. This new order was based on *Pancasila* (Five Pillars) of belief in one God, nationalism, international cooperation, democracy and social justice. Again, however, over centralization of government and control by a elite has led to both corruption and militarization. This is being challenged by democratic forces, one led by Megawati Sukarnoputri, daughter of former President Sukarno.

The Philippines Ferdinand Marcos transformed a fledgling democracy into a one man--one state country. Self-proclaimed savior of the nation, he ran for political office on the slogan "Rice and Roads" liberally spending money from the public treasury (and financed from the United States) His variety of constitutional authoritarianism became progressively elitist, corrupt, and divorced from reality. A political challenge was mounted by Senator Benigno Aquino. When Aquino was assassinated, a collage of forces organized a "people's movement." The result was a exhilarating transfer of the presidency to Corazon Aquino, wife of the martyred Benigno. A successful transition to the presidency of retired general Fidel Ramos was managed in 1992. The recent transition to a more democratic regime has been exciting. Whether or not the events of 1989 will produce a strong, legitimate democracy remains to be seen as many of the problems of elitism, militarism, and authoritarianism, remain.

Korean politics have been a combination of domestic forces and international (U.S.) influence. Post Korean War problems included the lack of a workable, legal framework for government, lack of political parties, a tradition of radialized opposition and a politicized military. In spite of these problems, Korea had a democratic revival of sorts in 1987 and has made significant progress towards a more representative and responsive government. Continuing problems stem from the issues of reunification and the continuing presence of U.S. military forces.

Areas of challenge listed by the authors include the political culture, historical and colonial legacies, ethnic and regional rivalries, state and society relationships, socioeconomic development and economic performance, international influences, and the leadership and the role of the military.

Outline

I. Power and Authority
    A. Differing conceptions but none reflect the European developmental model
        1. Japanese focus on relationships
        2. Chinese focus centrality
    B. Different resources and colonial experience
    C. Unity of ethics and order
    D. Elitist

II. Thailand
    A. Enlightened monarchy of King Chulalongkorn
        1. Constitutional regime to the time of the Japanese occupation (1932)
        2. Japanese surrender in 1945
        3. Reinstitution of National Assembly
    B. Military coups between 1951 and 1991
    C. Current situation
        1. King Bhuimbol and semi-democratic government
        2. Balance between military, Assembly, monarchy, middle class and business community now favors military
        3. Ideas of benevolent superior

III. Malaysia
    A. Population base
        1. Communal: Chinese and Malay
        2. Religious, economic, political, business differentiation
        3. Practice of Islam is both culturally Malay and Islamic
    B. Political evolution
        1. British colonialism
        2. Development of the Alliance Party
        3. May 1969 rioting and the National Operations Council
        4. Restoration of parliamentary democracy and the influence of *bumiputera*

    C. Dr. Mahthir Mohamad (1981)
        1. International Security Act
        2. Limiting a limited democracy

IV. Indonesia
    A. Population base
        1. Muslim but not an Islamic state
        2. Problems of the ethnic Chinese
        3. Remnants of Dutch colonialism
    B. Sukarno and "Guided Democracy"
        1. Principles of consensus decision making
        2. Disdain for minorities, intellectuals, and liberalism
        3. Government becomes corrupt and ineffective
    C. Internal war of 1966
        1. Blamed on the Communist Party (PKI) and ethnic minorities
        2. Causes include economic, military, political, and international factors
    D. Suharto
        1. The five pillars: belief in One God, nationalism, international cooperation, democracy and social justice
        2. GOLKAR
        3. The New Order
        4. Democracy an elusive goal
        5. Voice of dissent of Megawati Sukarnoputri, daughter of Sukarno

V. The Philippines: from independence to martial law, 1946 - 1972
    A. Old Order elite maintenance
    B. Rise of Ferdinand Marcos
        1. Nationalist agenda
        2. U.S. financial support
        3. Constitutional authoritarianism and over-reliance on the military
        4. Dissent and assassination of Benigno Aquino, (1983)
    C. "People power"
        1. Cardinal Sin

     2. Corazon Aquino
     3. Fidel Ramos, retired general, becomes president
   D. Remaining problems of class differences, special interests, militarism

VI. South Korea: the suppression of democracy, 1948 - 1987
   A. Problems
     1. Absence of workable, legal framework
     2. Lack of political parties
     3. Radicalized opposition
     4. Politicized military
   B. 1987 democratic revival
   C. Continuing problems
     1. Corruption
     2. Impact of the threat from North Korea and continued U.S. presence

VII. Taiwan
   A. Trouble with democratic liberalization
   B. Problems with relationship with the mainland

VIII. Hong Kong
   A. British transfer control to China, 1997
   B. Emigration
   C. Problems with democracy and economic independence

IX. Areas of challenge: political, colonial legacy, ethnic rivalries, state--society relationships, economic performances, international arena
   A. Political culture
   B. Historical and colonial legacies
   C. Ethnic and regional rivalries
   D. State and society
   E. Socioeconomic development and economic performance
   F. International influences
   G. Leadership and the military's role

Key Terms

dual function of the military
GOLKAR
Guided democracy
Pancasila
"one country, two systems"

Names

Chulalongkorn
King Bhuimbol
Aung San Suu Kyi
Dr. Mahthir Mohamad (1981)
Sukarno
Suharto
Megawati Sukarnoputri
Ferdinand Marcos
Benigno Aquino
Cardinal Sin
Fidel Ramos
Syngman Rhee

Key Concepts

abangan: Indonesian form of religion which combines elements of animism, Buddhism, Hinduism, and Islam

GOLKAR: A "functional group" as part of Sukarno's "Guided Democracy." It emphasis social mobilization for projects with broad national import by use of mass energy and labor.

guided democracy: a political form where presidential power was used to develop consensus and guide national policy as indicated in Indonesia.

limited democracy: As found in Malaysia, the military and other political elites limited popular participation in government to those activities not considered dangerous to the country's stability and development.

communal parties: political parties based entirely or in large part on ethnic group or 'communal' representation. It is an exclusionary rather than inclusionary form of representation in that one must belong to the group prior to belonging to the political party.

dual function of the military: an situation wherein the military is in charge of both external defense and internal security blurring any distinction between military and policing activities.

martial law: temporary rule by military authorities imposed upon a civilian population in time of war or when civil authorities have ceased to function.

People Power: an idea reflecting the development of grassroots movements against political repression. Particularly notable in the 1980s in the Philippines for its success in supporting the overthrow of the Marcos regime.

coup d'etat: the overthrow of government by a small, elite group generally involving only limited violence.

enlightened, or benevolent monarchy: a king or ruler with absolute power who believes, or seeks to act in the interests of the entire population rather than in the interests of the elite.

Knowledge, understanding and evaluation

1. One of the more interesting points the author makes is that Asian and Western conceptions of change differ significantly. The Chinese may emphasize centrality and balance while the Japanese focus on human relationships, but neither conceptualize change as "progress" or "development." This has important ramifications for the dialogue between the U.S. and its Asian allies.

2. The overseas Chinese, whether in Malaysia, Indonesia or Singapore, are both

economically powerful and political vulnerable.

3. There is a wide range of military philosophies concerning the nature of the relationship between the military and society. This is especially significant in Thailand where the military sees itself as part of society not as repressive of society. Although it is not the elitism of class, it is a form of elite management from the top down.

4. This chapter does not focus on the experiences of these countries during the Japanese occupation and what changes that effected, if any.

5. Islam in Malaysia is a state religion where in Indonesia it is not an official religion. This may or may not reflect the power of Islam and the activities of radical elements.

6. The groups called "Islamic fundamentalists" may be simply political groups who have formed in opposition to oppressive rule who also happen to be Islamic. There is little indication that these Sunni groups have an agenda which includes the institution of Sharia.

7. The reunification of Hong Kong with the rest of mainland China was a difficult international problem. It also poses significant difficulties for Taiwan.

8. Reunification of South Korea and North Korea is an inevitability. What this means for continued U.S. involvement in the area remains to be seen.

9. The influence of the United States in the region is probably exaggerated. It is generally easier to blame an outside imperialist force than to take remedial domestic measures to solve internal political problems

10. In spite of the problems discussed in this chapter, each of the governments are under both domestic and international pressure to become more responsible to their populations.

Topics for Research Papers

1. The Monarchy of Thailand as a Force for Democracy
2. The Nobel Peace Prize of Aung San Suu Kyi
3. Communal Politics of Malaysia
4. The Formation of the Alliance Party of Indonesia
5. Corazon Aquino and "People Power"
6. The Effect

CHAPTER 9

Sentimental Imperialists: America in Asia

Overview

The title, "Sentimental Imperialists" is fitting. Americans have had both a moral and philosophical attachment to China, Korea, and Vietnam as well as exhibiting some of those behaviors associated with other imperialist powers. Early associations with Asian countries had been generally benevolent as is seen in earlier chapters in this text. Early in this century (immigration policy to the contrary) American influence in Asia was limited to missionary efforts, educators, liberal thinkers and a few business people. After the worlds' turn in the 1930s, a combination of economic depression and the rise of an alternative political form -- communism, this benevolent attitude changed to one that was more protective of self-interests. U.S. foreign policy became built around the concept of "containment" as outlined by George Kennan.

The general policy of containment was given force by the Truman Doctrine which basically stated that the United States would fight communism whenever and wherever necessary to fight its spread. The NSC-68 added a rationale of the "balance of power" further supporting an oppositional stance to communism. When China, Korea, and eventually Vietnam were "lost," it was seen as major policy failure.

Ideology was seen as the single most powerful motivating force. The fight between democratic and communist forces in China was given as evidence of the terrible effects of possible battles between the forces for good and evil. This was in spite of the efforts of some of the China specialists in the U.S. State Department who argued otherwise. The Kuomintang lost for several reasons including the failure of external support, internal fragmentation of the KDP, and the lack of strong ideological commitment.

When Korea was threatened, the U.S. was determined not to let another domino fall so much so that the U.S. Army created the U.S. Army Military Government in Korea (USAMGIK). U.S. Soviet rivalry in the division of the peninsula (1945) eventually meant that a line was drawn at the thirty eighth parallel separating the communist and democratic forces. The Korean War, the forgotten war, lasted between 1950 and 1953. The United States has had a military, economic and political presence in Korea since that time. Pressure for reunification is increasing but the DMZ remains one of the most militarily congested pieces of real estate in the world.

The story of the United States and Vietnam is truly sad for both countries. The Vietnamese suffered in the First Indo-China War (with France) and absorbed the casualties and costs of the Second Indo-China War with the United States. Each U.S. president -- Eisenhower, Truman, Kennedy and Johnson -- took an active interest in support the forces for freedom against the forces of communism in Vietnam. The motivation was reasonably straightforward and based simply on the assumption that communism enslaved people and that the countries of South and South East Asia would fall like dominos if they were not supported by the free world. The United States became increasingly involved in the convoluted politics of South Vietnam and was later entrenched in a war. The conflict ended as a result of two factors: (1) the United States lost its political resolve as a result of covert activities inconsistent with a democracy, and (2) the corruption of the South Vietnamese government left the U.S. fighting for an 'unworthy' ally. The Paris Peace talks and subsequent withdrawal of U.S. troops led to reunification in 1975.

The United States remains a Pacific power. Benefits to the region of Pax Americana have been in reducing the cost of security and maintaining a military force which deterred minor aggressive activities. This is changing both as a result of the U.S. being unwilling to continue shouldering the enormous cost of military hegemony and as a result of the region's newly acquired abilities to support regional alliances. The question of replacement of the "nuclear umbrella" remains significant. In the meantime, capitalism remains triumphant and political dialogue the preferred strategy.

Outline

I. Basis of U.S. foreign policy
    A. Benevolent missionaries, educators and liberal thinkers
    B. Wilsonian principles undermined by economic crisis of the 1930s
    C. U.S. policy and doctrine
        1. George Kennan and the policy of containment of communism
        2. Replaced Wilsonian goals of human rights and self determination
        3. The Truman Doctrine and military implications
    D. Loss of China, Korea, and Vietnam to non-democratic forces
    E. NSC-68 and the balance of power as rationale
    F. Hegemony and the transfer of power responsibilities

II. China
    A. World War II emphasis on Japan left democratic forces in China without allies
    B. The loss of China, the Cold War, and fear of communism
    C. Failure of the Kuomintang (KMT)
    D. Unsatisfactory explanation for American people
        1. John Foster Dulles
        2. Madame Chaing
        3. The purge of the China lobby

III. Korea
    A. The Domino Theory
    B. U.S. Army Military Government in Korea (USAMGIK)
    C. U.S. Soviet Rivalry in the division of the peninsula (1945)

        D.   The Korean War (1950 - 1953)
                1.   The thirty-eighth parallel
                2.   DPRK versus the ROK
                3.   General Douglas MacArthur

IV.   Vietnam
        A.   The Geneva Agreement, 1954 and division along the seventeenth parallel
        B.   U.S. Presidents Eisenhower, Truman, Kennedy and Johnson
        C.   Regional motivation, the domino theory
        D.   Internal motivation, support for democracy and freedom
        E.   The Military Assistance Command Vietnam (MACV) (1961 - 1962)
        F.   War
        G.   Paris Peace talks and withdrawal
        H.   Reunification in 1975

V.   Summary and conclusions
        A.   Change to regional balance of power from military hegemony of the United States
        B.   Benefits of Pax Americana
        C.   Important U.S. strategists included Edward Lansdale, Henry Kissinger, and George Kennan
                1.   Costs borne by U.S.
                2.   Nuclear umbrella may be forestalled nuclear proliferation in the region
                3.   Political rapproachement
        D.   Triumphant capitalism

Terms
Domino Theory
Truman Doctrine
Kuomintang (KMT)
Pax Americana
collective security
nuclear umbrella
NSC-68
rapprochement

Names
George Kennan
Edward Lansdale
Henry Kissinger
Madame Chaing
Syngman Rhee

Key Concepts

containment: The U.S. policy of containment sought to block Soviet expansionism in the world by a variety of political, economic and social means.

McCarthyism: The term refers both to the scare tactics (accusations of being communist or communist sympathizers) used by Senator Joe McCarthy to build a political base and fear of the spread of communism which led to an atmosphere of political hysteria in the United States.

alliances: political agreements between and among soverieng states meant to increase cooperative economic, political, and diplomatic activities to the benefit of all parties.

Truman Doctrine: The policy of "supporting free peoples who are resisting attempted subjugation by armed minorities or outside pressures" as advocated by John Foster Dulles and President Harry S Truman.

loss of China: China's revolution and movement to communism was variously blamed on the State Department, the President, and various ambassadors leading to politically motivated purges in each of the branches of the U.S. government.

American Occupation of Korea (USAMGIK): Military rule by the United States government subsequent to World War II which was supportive of social and economic reform while simultaneously supportive of conservative political arrangements.

domino theory: the assumption that the countries of South Asia would 'fall like dominoes' if American power was not used on the first line of defense.

rapprochement: leading to better relationships between countries.

normalization: Normalization of diplomatic relationships occurs when countries formally exchange ambassadors and establish embassies in the respective countries.

NSC-68: formal policy document of the United States which forwarded the proposition that the balance of power between the USSR and the United States depended upon both the perception and the reality of power.

Knowledge, understanding and evaluation

1. Understand the underlying motivation for U.S. involvement changed over the course of time from one of assumed benevolence to realpolitik.

2. The domino theory was taken very seriously by those who understood the power of an idea.

3. There was a significant split in the U.S. government over China policy which resulted in a purging of State Department "China hands" i.e., experts.

Individuals who had spent their entire professional careers studying and understanding China were supplanted by those who were ideologically motivated.

4. The Korean War is the "forgotten war." Motivations for U.S. involvement were clearly mixed. Note that the U.S. army actually set up a government for southern Korea as it had for the Philippines. This is seen as wrong-headed in contemporary military doctrine. (Somalia, Bosnia, and Cambodia are examples of where it could have happened and didn't.

5. The CIA played an important role in the shaping of the early days of the Vietnam War. Covert activities were evaluated as being a necessary tool to combat the forces of communism.

6. Drawing lines to separate neighbors only changes the place they may fight. The thirty-eighth parallel and the seventeenth parallel were meant to separate protagonists. The lines became the focus of fighting.

7. The Vietnam War was tragic for the people of Vietnam. They had a high number of casualties and paid a high penalty. For the United States, the penalty was different. It was not only the deaths more than 58,000 individuals, but a loss of direction and respect for government.

8. American prestige and reputation were damaged by some of the actions in China, Korea, and Vietnam, although American motivation and ideology are still admired.

9. The Korean government has yet to become a legitimate, transparent democracy.

10. Rapprochement between the United States and Vietnam is proceeding slowly but surely.

Topics for Research Papers

1. Edward Lansdale and the CIA in Vietnam

2. The U.S. and the U.N. in Korea
3. Chinese and U.S.S.R. Support for North Korea
4. The New American Embassy in Ho Chi Minh City
5. The Mining of the DeMilitarized Zone in Korea
6. The Future of North Korea
7. John Paul Vann and the Bright Shining Lie
8. President Truman and Douglas MacArthur
9. The Story of Syngman Rhee
10. From Formosa to Taiwan

CHAPTER 10

China's Long March Toward Modernization

Overview

The first part of this chapter contains an extensive chronology of events in China between 1949 and the late 1990s. It is a representative of the dynamic tension between traditional Chinese culture and forces for modernization. It is also illustrative of the tension between those who would support a more open, free and democratic China and those who maintain that stability and progress must be managed and controlled. Tian'anmen Square remains a poignant symbol representing the establishment of the revolutionary People's Republic of China on October 1, 1948 and the repression of a people's revolution at the same place, May 20, 1989.

Noted liberal philosopher, Fang Lizhi, writes on the theme of "Chinese amnesia" contending that the ruling authorities are prone to forget the philosophical basis of revolutionary struggle and repress those who 'struggle.' He gives a number of examples of what might be called "selective amnesia" of party members. He also implies that scholar and expert, Edgar Snow, was part of the "Special Propaganda Department" when, for example, he did not recognize the 1960s famine where twenty-five million people died.

Contributor Harry Harding discusses the imperative to political reform the Chinese government has attempted in the 1980s. The intellectual imperative was to balance the role of ideology with that of pragmatism. From Maoism to

Deng Xiaoping's call to "Seek truth from facts," the role of ideology has been controversial. The second imperative is political. The tension has been between those who support strong central control and those realize that central repressive forces often short-circuit necessary feedback and corrective measures. Understanding the economic imperative is critical. Chinese leaders understand that China not only has a fragile infrastructure but that over dependence on the outside world could tip the balance. The climate and geography of China provide special difficulties as evidenced in the number of famines, crop failures and regional resource shortages. Five steps were suggested to integrate political and economic reform: (1) reorganization of the bureaucracy to make it more compatible with the needs of economic development, (2) modernization of the civil service, (3) decentralization of administrative power, (4) creation of a more rational policy-making process, and (5) a reduced role for the Chinese Communist Party in routine political and economic affairs. These have been inconsistently and ineffectively applied as a result of the hold of the old party leadership. The societal imperative is also interesting. Harding suggests that the removal of political and class labels, the relaxation of political controls over details of daily life, and the establishment of easier modes of communication between political leaders and citizens, would lead to the revitalization and restructuring of society's relationship with the government. These were a dangerous blend of success and failure.

Challenges to the Chinese economic system remain. The leadership agrees that reform of price and the factor markets through indirect control is critical. They also know that these changes require political courage because those who would lose as a result of the reforms are often powerful players in the political system. The fundamental economic problems stem from regional disparities, agricultural production, employment opportunities, urbanization and competitive pricing. A proper balance in trade relationships with the international community is difficult to achieve under these conditions.

Another significant problem area for the economic, political and societal sectors is that of demographics. Chinese policy has ranged from financial support for large families to financial support for controlling birth. The relationship between the number of people, the resources of the country and popular demand for consumer goods may prove incendiary. Urbanization not only present the familiar challenges but in China, the numbers are swollen by a substantial "floating population." Unemployment is high as a result of two factors: (1) the large number of first-time job seekers and, (2) the number of people moving out of the labor-intensive agricultural occupations.

Other issues discuss in the chapter of continuing interest are the influence of religion, western cultural imperialism, reforms of school curriculum, cultural dilemmas, the influence of technological improvement, art and music and the continuing transformation of Chinese culture.

Outline

I. Chronology
    A. The struggle between order and disorder; control and freedom
    B. Symbolism of Tian'anmen Square

II. Chinese amnesia
    A. Fang Lizhi
    B. Ability and requirement of forgetting the lessons of history

III. Imperatives
    A. Intellectual imperative to balance the role of ideology and pragmatism
    B. Political imperative to balance to role of control and freedom
    C. Economic imperative to balance domestic and international factors
    D. Need to integrate political and economic reform
        1. Reorganize bureaucracy
        2. Modernize civil service
        3. Decentralize administrative power
        4. Create a more rational policy-making process
        5. Reduce the role of the Party in routine political and economic affairs
    E. Societal imperative
        1. Removal of political and class labels
        2. Relaxation of political controls over details of daily life

        3. Establishing modes of communication between leaders and citizens
IV. Challenges to the economic system
    A. Regional disparities
    B. Agricultural production
    C. Employment and labor problems
    D. Urbanization
    E. Market pricing
    F. International trade relationships
V. Challenges to the political and social system
    A. Demographics
    B. Urbanization
    C. Floating population
    D. Unemployment
VI. Current issues
    A. Fertility control
    B. Influence of religion
    C. Reform of the school system
    D. Support for technological improvement
    E. Western influence in art, music
    F. The transformation of Chinese culture
    G. Western cultural imperialism

Terms
Tian'anmen Square
Mandate of Heaven
People's Republic of China (PRC)
Five Year plans
collectivization plans
CCP
Cultural Revolution
Red Guard
The Gang of Four
fertility control

Names
Deng Xiaoping
Mao Zedong
Hu Yaobang
Zao Ziyang
Fang Lizhi
Edgar Snow

Key Concepts

Maoism: A philosophy of continuous revolution based on concepts proposed by MaoZedong. The components were peasant leadership, rural agrarian bases, anti-intellectualism, mass movements, purges of counter revolutionaries, and the destruction of class differentials.

cadre: member of the Communist Party.

rightist: In Chinese terms, individuals who supported traditional Chinese culture and government.

struggle: The assumption that the masses must work intellectually and physically to overcome traditional thought and behavior.

proletarian dictatorship: the idea that the working people of the country had the right and responsibility to 'dictate' the policies of the government.

mixed system: socialism with Chinese characteristics was to include both government planning and individual enterprise.

demographic changes: Changes in the number, distribution, welfare, rate of increase of the population of a country which serve to indicate the level of social-economic welfare.

fertility policy: Policy meant to control the number of pregnancies, live births, and/ or population growth rate of a country.

cultural dilemma: The problems faced by individuals and countries in trying to retain cultural integrity in the face of modernization and development which tend to undercut traditional loyalties while supporting a higher living standard.

State Owned Enterprises (SOE): Selling, or privatizing, companies owned by the government is a problem in finding buyers with sufficient capital, management experience and profit motivation. There is also an issue involved with public goods produced by some of the larger state owned industries and the inability of people to pay the price as set by the industry considering the decreasing level of extractive capabilities of the state..

Knowledge, understanding and evaluation

1. This period of Chinese history is one of instability and dramatic change.

2. This period of instability and change also reflects Chinese traditional beliefs and social practices.

3. Influences from the outside, whether technological or ideological, have deeply affected China.

4. Political and economic reform must be tangential.

5. When political and economic reform do not proceed together, there will be serious failures in one or both dimensions.

6. The leadership of China is changing from leaders who were influenced by the Long March and the Cultural Revolution to younger leadership whose experience is with bureaucratization and institutionalization of revolutionary principles.

7. Chinese leaders are well aware of the problems of over-centralization and command economies. The basic problem is the over-centralization of the political system. Centralization without corrections from the periphery will eventually skew the entire process.

8. Chinese people may be infinitely better off economically than they were before the Revolution. This comparative statement does not indicate that they are satisfied with the rate and direction of change.

9. The forces for democracy will continue to propel the country towards increased openness and responsiveness. This will be as a partial result of the inability of any country to control modern communication.

10. China will increasingly play a major role in the region as both producer and market.

Topics for Research Papers

1. Comparing Mao's Long March and the Long March to Modernization
2. China's Population Programs
3. Trading Relationships between China and Japan
4. Tian'amen Square
5. The Modernization of the Chinese Military
6. The Relationship between the People's Revolutionary Army and the People's Republic of China
7. Edgar Snow and Mao Zedong
8. Tibet
9. The Over-Seas Chinese in SouthAsian Politics
10. Ethnic Minorities of China

CHAPTER 11

Beyond the Revolution: Indonesia and Vietnam

Overview

This chapter focuses on the two countries that have had the most important impact on the political affairs of the region and the roles of the external powers. Indonesia's size and wealth of resources contributed to its centrality; Vietnam's role in the Cold War made it an important factor in external relationships. They are similar in that the fight for independence took a revolutionary form in both countries but subsequent events led each to take a different path.

Indonesia won its independence from the Dutch in December of 1949 after a protracted guerrilla war. Even after political independence had been achieved, economic independence and development remained very much under the control of Dutch companies. President Sukarno believed that Western imperialism had to be directly confronted and took economic, military and political measures to counter Dutch, British and U.S. efforts in the region -- even taking on Malaysia and Singapore. Internally, he launched a nationalistic economic and political program called "Guided Democracy."

The events of 1965 produced one of the most significant political shifts in Asia and the Pacific in the postwar period. The country did a dramatic volte-face in its internal politics turning from communism to a nationalistic, centralized, dictatorship under President Suharto. Relationships with the Chinese became strained both as a result of the change from communism and the treatment of overseas Chinese living in Indonesia. Technically, Indonesia was nonaligned; formally it had strong relationships with Vietnam. The new internal policy was called the "New Order" and its programs characterized by an emphasis on growth and development of the economy while remaining under the political control of the president, ruling elites, and military hierarchy. There was a strong relationship between the military and the political leadership as indicated in the organization, Golkar, that claimed to be a civil association. Suharto was able to maintain this arrangement by apportioning the monies accrued from the petroleum and agricultural export economy. At the end of the 1960's the economy experienced a rapid growth in both the export sector and the country was self-sufficient in rice production. Petroleum accounted for 65 percent of all export earnings.

Foreign policy during the 1960's was clearly based on perceived Indonesian self-interest. Relationships with communist countries were cool and cordial; relationships with the west could be characterized and warm but cautious, and relationships with the international order were strained by the invasions and incorporation of East Timor (1974). The United States became a major supplier of military training and equipment but avoided commitment to a bilateral defense arrangement.

By the end of the 1970s, Suharto's New Order was firmly established. Even in the political arena, Suharto managed to balance Golkar with the Moslem-based United Development Party (PPP). Under the doctrine of Dwi Fungsi (dual function) the military was accorded both military and social-political duties. The regime's accomplishments are notable and include agricultural production, significant improvements in health and education, family planning and rural infrastructure development. It continues to be criticized for lack of a transparent democracy, treatment of minorities, and the high level of military involvement in the political arena. Indonesia's relationships with China may be characterized as wary pragmatism.

<u>Vietnam</u> won its independence from the French after defeating them at Dien Bien Phu in May of 1954. Unlike Indonesia, the peace that followed split the

country in two. The Geneva conference left the north under the control of the Communist Viet Minh forces led by Ho Chi Minh. In the South, the Republic of Vietnam was established as a separate pro-American administration. The National Liberation Front (NLF) was founded in 1960 to destabilized the regime of Ngo Dinh Diem. Diem's assassination triggered United States' involvement in the country. Covert action became overt military involvement after the Tonkin Gulf Incident. President Lyndon Johnson ordered the first air attacks on North Vietnam and regular U.S. combat units arrived in Da Nang by the summer of 1965.

The South Vietnamese regime fell in April of 1975 and the country was taken over by the <u>Provisional Revolutionary Government.</u> Hanoi clearly underestimated the political will and economic resources necessary to reunite the country. On July 2, 1976, the country was formally reunified as the Socialist Republic of Vietnam (SRV) and a program of industrialization and socialization of the economy was adopted. The population was alienated and by 1978 tens of thousands of Vietnamese became the "boat people." Vietnam invaded Cambodia in 1978 for two major reasons: (1) border incursions threatened the stability of the country, and (2) the Kymer Rouge led by Pol Pot was odious to the entire international community. Vietnam installed the People's Republic of Kampuchia in Phnom Penh led by Heng Samrin. This provided a dilemma for the international state system. One the one hand, they could not countenance the return of the Kymer Rouge, but on the other hand, Vietnamese "imperialism" was equally distasteful. China responded with a border incursion meant to be symbolically threatening. The Cambodians resisted and the international community (ASEAN and the UN) supported a new government, the Coalition Government of Democratic Kampuchea (CGDK). Vietnam retreated and reestablished closer ties with the Soviet government eventually granting them base facilities at Da Nang and Cam Ranh Bay.

Internally, Vietnam took on a reform program in 1987 attempting new economic and social programs. Vietnam again became a net exporter of rice. Even restrictions on religious practice were lifted. Foreign policy became more open to outside influence. The economy began to grow and develop. However, political reform did not accompany economic progress and by the mid 1990s the government elites had moved to reestablish firm control over the country.

In conclusion, Indonesia and Vietnam are similar in that they reject notions of Western liberal democracy, have authoritarian and centralized governments, and have militaries which are heavily involved in politics. They differ most markedly in the fact that Indonesia has relatively more successful economically.

Outline

I. Focus
    A. Impact of revolution
    B. Differences in size and wealth
    C. External relationships

II. Indonesia
    A. Sukarno's Guided Democracy (1949 - 1965)
        1. Nationalism guides both domestic and international politics
        2. Ends with bloody revolution
    B. President Suharto and the "New Order"
        1. Political base a combination of military and elites
        2. Domestic programs
            a. Successful in economic growth and development based on petroleum and agricultural exports
            b. Political restraint and formation of Golkar
        3. Foreign policy
            a. Distrust of China
            b. Cool and controlled relationships with West
            c. Problems stemming from invasion of East Timor

III. Vietnam
    A. Impact of revolution
        1. Defeat of French at Dien Bien Phu (1954)
        2. Division of country by Geneva conference
            a. South: Ngo Dinh Diem
            b. North: Ho Chi Minh
        3. War with United States

		a.	Tonkin Gulf Incident

          a.   Tonkin Gulf Incident
          b.   U.S. troops in Da Nang (1965)
    4.   End of war 1975
          a.   Establishment as Socialist Republic of Vietnam
          b.   Political and economic problems of reunification
    5.   Vietnam's invasion of Cambodia
          a.   Repel Pol Pot and the Khymer Rouge
          b.   Installation of Heng Samrin
          c.   China's reaction and border incursion
          d.   International dilemma
    6.   New reform programs of 1987 reversed in mid 1990s

IV. Summary
    A.   Similarities in rejection of Western liberal democracy, centralization of government and military involvement in politics
    B.   Differences largely stemming from Indonesia's economic resources.

Key Terms

Terms	Names	Places
Guided Democracy	Sukarno	Da Nang
New Order	Suharto	Dien Bien Phu
Pertamina	Lyndon Baines	Ho Chi Minh City
Dwi Fungsi	Johnson	Saigon
Golkar	Ngo Dinh Diem	Hanoi
Kymer Rouge	Ho Chi Minh	Jakarta
Viet Minh	General Benny	
Viet Cong	Murdani	
Tonkin Incident	Heng Samrin	
Cam Ranh Bay	Pol Pot	

Key Concepts

<u>protracted guerrilla war</u>: a war which is assumed to be winnable only as a war of attrition, i.e., a war which wears down the resolve of the opponent.

<u>covert American involvement</u>: covert activities in South Asia were conducted under the auspices of the Central Intelligence Agency and other agencies of the U.S. government. These agencies are responsible to Congress and covert activites were checked when it became apparent that they were counter-productive in the field and antagonistic to the basic framework of the American Constitution.

<u>purges:</u> a program of cleansing, i.e., in social terms, these refers to the elimination of populations deemed unclean or polluting to the larger population. Tactics of governments may include deportation, expulsion, genocide, and/or ethnic cleansing.

<u>military dominance</u>: Until the end of the Cold War, it was assumed that preponderance of sheer technological weight and power insured battlefield success which was based on the holding of territory. Most countries built up their military power after calculating their particular 'security dilemma.' In a modern context, this may no longer be the case.

<u>student radical</u>: Student radicals in Asia have often been both the impetus and the tool of political change. The term 'radical' can refer to any position which is diametrically opposed to the official position of the government - either that of the left or right.

<u>foreign capital</u>: Monies which flow into one country from another. These monies may be invested in a number of ways but always effect the value of currency within the recipient country.

<u>passive resistance</u>: an emphasis on nonviolent tactics as the most effective means of reaching a given social or political objective.

<u>genocide:</u> the intentional destruction of a people either through expulsion, direct

killing, control of fertility, or elimination of the means of survival. Formally defined in the United Nation's Convention on Genocide (1956)

<u>new people/ base people</u>: terms which refer to the peasantry or those groups not in control of the political mechanisms of the state. In benevolent or not-so-benevolent dictatorship, actions are often taken on behalf of the 'people' which may or may not benefit the intended recipients.

Knowledge, understanding and evaluation

1. The revolutionary experience of both Indonesia and Vietnam predisposed the population to distrust of foreign intervention in internal political affairs. This distrust is evident even in contemporary foreign policy.

2. Communism and nationalism competed for ideological dominance in the region. It is fair to say that nationalism eventually "won" but that the ideas of socialism which were congruent with indigenous practices, were also accepted.

3. Vietnam's activities in Cambodia presented a important dilemma for the international community. It could not sanction a country's invasion of another country and yet no other nation had taken significant actions to counter the brutality of the Pol Pot regime.

4. The United States' involvement in Vietnam had different domestic consequences for Vietnam than it had for the United States. In Vietnam, it was a continuation of colonial, imperialistic French rule. In the United States the questions concerned the government's relationship to the people as well as the motivations and nature of U.S. foreign policy.

5. The history of Indonesia is not complete. It remains to be seen whether the 1998 recession will have significant political as well as economic effects.

6. These countries present clear illustrations of the problems incumbent with significant levels of military influence on government. The experiment with Golkar meant to 'socialize' the military is unique.

7. An interesting study could be made comparing the First, Second and Third Indo-China War. Were the causes similar and/or related? Was the nature of the fighting itself the same i.e., civilian casualties, use of weaponry, financial support, external involvement?

8. The authors mention journalistic and press activities in each of the descriptions of political protest. Literacy, intellectuals and education present a formidable challenge to conservative governments who must have an educated labor force for the country to develop but know that an educated labor force also demands a responsible and responsive government.

9. There seems to be some fear of liberal democracy in some of the Asian countries. This may not be different than fear of liberal democracy anywhere else in the world. (And, probably not much different than the fear of democracy as elucidated by James Madison, Alexander Hamilton, and even Thomas Jefferson.)

10. One of the basic questions of Chapter 10 was concerning the relationship between political and economic development. Both Indonesia and Vietnam provide illustrations of the difficulties encountered when they do not proceed in tandem.

Topics for Research Papers

1. The French Experience in Vietnam
2. How did the French Experience in Vietnam differ from the American Experience?
3. Vietnam as a Colonial Power in Cambodia.
4. The Legacy of Pol Pot.
5. Petroleum and The Relationship between Indonesia and Japan
6. The Tet Offensive
7. The Tonkin Gulf Incident
8. Comparing Sukarno and Suharto
9. Indonesia and the Bangdung Conference
10. Landmines in Cambodia

CHAPTER 12

Siberian Salient: Russia in Pacific Asia

Overview

This area is not very well known nor appreciated by Westerners in spite of its great size, location, abundance of natural resources, and importance to the future of the Pacific region. Understanding the geography and climate of the area is crucial: three fourths of USSR is in Asia and a third of Asia is in USSR The Northern Territories are former Japanese islands occupied by Soviets since 1945 and provide a source of continued tension between the two regional powers. Russia's problems in the area stem from the extreme distance of 3,100 miles from Korea to Bering Strait, differences in culture, historical invasion of Western Russia by Eastern Russia and an extraordinarily long coastline which is difficult to control.

Historically, Russia had a number of confrontations with both China and Japan. As early as 1689, the Chinese expelled Russians from the Amer. Valley and were forced to sign the Treaty of Nerchinsk. Later, under Peter the Great, Russia tried to exert more effective control over the region through a series of military and exploratory expeditions (1725-1750) Part of the motivation was the exploitation of furs which eventually led to almost total depletion of the natural stock. The "Siberian Railway" from Manchuria to Vladivostok was an additional effort to extend Russian control. The Russo-Japanese War ended badly for the Russians but after they reexerted control over the region, it provided a base for Cominterm operations between 1923 and 1941. The Stalin era had two major effects on the region: Balkanization and the institution of labor camps. Neither were positive experiences for indigenous peoples nor public perceptions of the region. The border control regimes have been particularly brutal and confrontational. Mikhail Gorbachev, repeating initiatives by other Soviet leaders, declared a Vladivostok Initiative in 1986 which was meant to build a more harmonious relationship between the government and the people and set the stage for the region's more effective political and economic integration into the Pacific arena.

This region will be increasingly important as its rich natural resources are exploited by Japan, China, the United States and Russia. Administrative control will continue to be a problem for Russia as it is in national interests to retain control of the natural resources and Pacific coastline.

Outline

I. Overlooked area by Westerners
II. Geography
    A. Three fourths of USSR is in Asia
    B. Third of Asia is in USSR
    C. Northern Territories are former Japanese islands occupied by Soviets since 1945
    D. 3,100 miles from Korea to Bering Strait
    E. Water coastline
III. Early history of confrontation with China
    A. Treaty of Nerchinsk (1689) expelled Russians from Amer. Valley
    B. Peoples of area - Koryaks, Chukchi, Tlingits
IV. Russian influence in the area
    A. Expeditions under Peter the Great 1725-1750
    B. Russian American Company as a trading monopoly for fur exploitation
    C. Railroad from Manchuria to Vladivostok
    D. Russo-Japanese War

	E.	Base for Cominterm operations 1923-1941
	F.	Balkanization by Stalin 1938-1956
	G.	Siberian labor camps
	H.	Gorbachev's Vladivostok Initiative (1988+)
V.	Historical myths	
	A.	Disputed and historicized by Russia, Japan, and Korea
	B.	U.S. involvement and continuing interests
	C.	Historical continuity in Vladivostok Initiative
	D.	Russian invasions from East (Tartars, Cossack, Manchus, etc.)
	E.	175 uniformed border guards indicate possible national paranoia
VI.	Contemporary place	
	A.	Balkanized regionalism
	B.	Place in Pacific community initiatives
	C.	Economic development and exploitation of natural resources

Key Terms	**Places**	**Dates**
Koryaks	Siberia salient	1689 Treaty of
Chukchi	Kurile Islands	Nerchinsk
Cossacks	Northern Territories	Far Eastern
Russian American	Lake Baikal	Republic (1920)
Company	Muscovy	1988 glasnost
soviet *kollektiv*	Vladivostok	
Vladivostok	Golden Horn	
Initiative		

Key Concepts

<u>apparatchik</u>: government functionary. In the Far East, control over regional authorities was problematic because of the great distances and inherent difficulties in communication and transportation. This often implied corruption and misrule.

<u>bolshevik:</u> refers to the Communist insurgency and later the Communist Party

and its followers.

glasnost: An initiative largely attributed to Mikhail Gorbachev emphasizing openness or transparency of government.

perestroika: an initiative largely attributed to Mikhail Gorbachev, it emphasized reforming of government institutions.

red/ white Russian: The 'Reds' were the Bolsheviks, while 'white' refers to supporters of the Czar. Many of the conflicts between the groups took place East of the Ural Mountains.

Vladivostok Initiative: An intiative formally by Mikhail Gorbachev that was meant to emphasize the importance of the Far East in Russian affairs.

territorial expanse: Russia is 6,000 miles wide. This vast distance makes infrastructural support difficult and political control challenging.

chauvinist and revanchist: Chauvinism is the belief in the superiority of one's own group, however defined; revanchism is a movement to regain territory previously lost. Together, in this region, they refer to Russian attempts to foist both history and Russian culture on the Far East.

border guards. Russian border guards are tasked to control immigration and emigration along a vast border. An almost impossible task, it is often pursued with marginally legal tactics.

center-periphery: This dicotomy refers to the problems incumbent in communication between centralized government and outlying districts.

Knowledge, understanding and evaluation

1. This region of the world is not well known, understood or appreciated by Westerners.

2. The Russia has had difficulty in exerting effective administrative control in the region as a consequence of difficulties of space and distance as well as cultural differences. There is a long history of repression and corrupt political control in the region.

3. The regional borders with China, Japan and the United States are problematic and contentious.

4. Vladivostok has placed an important role in Russian maritime activities.

5. The region will be increasingly integrated into the Pacific Century as its natural resources are exploited by world powers.

Topics for Research Papers

1. Vladivostok, Russia's Route to the Pacific Century
2. The Siberian Railway
3. Stalin's Siberian Labor Camps
4. The Natural Resources of Siberia
5. Nuclear Testing in the Region
6. Japan-Russian Contention over the Kurile Islands
7. The Environment Problems of Lake Baikal
8. The Russian-American Company.
9. The Indigenous Peoples of the Region
10. The History of the Russian Orthodox Church in Alaska

CHAPTER 13

Pacific Century: Regional and Global Perspectives

Overview

This chapter summarizes the major findings in the text, provides an analysis of the contemporary situation and attempts to direct the student's attention to the future of the region.

At the beginning of the Pacific Century the region was is an era of rapid and unsettling change from a region with a high amount of poverty, an economic base built on agriculture and suffering from the remnants of colonialism. By the last decade of the century, it has virtually eliminated the worst of the poverty, has a solid industrial base, and governments that espouse principles of democracy if not the form.

There are two integrative frameworks: (1) regional, and (2) global. With regard to regional integration, economic and political relationships between and among the countries are solid, growing and mutually dependent. Global integration, particularly of financial markets will be increasingly important on the international scene.

The authors concentrate on economic development of the region from the period of reconstruction after World War II and the inception of Bretton Woods institutions such as GATT. It became a period of strong economic growth propelled by the strength and size of the U.S. market and was only temporarily stalled by the energy crisis of the 1970s. During the later part of the century, the impact of currency, globalization of large private firms, percentage of world trade share, and change of economic strategies, have been important.

Japan continues to have a uniquely important role in the region. It was an engine for growth for the NIEs and has special relationships with China, Thailand, and Indonesia. Relationships are tied i.e. are based on a type of *keiretsu* structure of tied economic dependency relationships even when it is in the form of international aid. Japan sees the region as a kind of spreading "V" with Japan at the point and the lesser developed countries following and gaining information and insight as to how it is to be done. Not all of the countries of Asia share this vision. China may take a lead position in the next century.

Asian global relationships have been traditionally built on economic relationships. It has generally had large trade surpluses, an emphasis on financial markets and technological development. Security for the region has been framed as economic security; military security may become more important in the future as the U.S. role is less dominant. There are strong and growing trade relationships with Europe, Latin America and Africa.

The period has been one of progress with regard to the reduction of poverty although pockets remain in southeast Asia and some of the island territories. Education, welfare, and health have improved. Lack of sufficient infrastructure, control of internal migration, population density, environmental degradation, AIDs, and other problems continue to challenge the region.

The authors conclude with a discussion of whether and how Asia differs from the rest of the world. In a brief section, they discuss cultural values built on Confucian sensibilities, technology for the benefit of the entire society and support for more equal distribution of welfare. What is certain, is that the region will continue to be fascinating as well as important to all who wish to watch.

Outline

I. Major developments in this century
   A. From poverty, inequality and underdevelopment
   B. Colonialism
   C. Reconstruction after World War II
      1. Bretton Woods institutions
      2. Strong economic growth
      3. Energy crisis of the 1970s
   D. Early stimulus of U.S. market
   E. Impact of currency values
   F. Globalization of large private firms
   G. World trade share of APEC now stands at 37 percent

II. Japan's role in the Asia-Pacific economy
   A. Regional expansion in the 1980s
   B. Support for the NIEs
   C. Relationships with other countries
      1. China and others
      2. Based on type of *keiretsu* structure of economic dependency
      3. Tied aid to China, Indonesia and Thailand
      4. "V" model of technical and economic progress

III. China
   A. High volume of trade between Japan and China
   B. Entrance via Hong Kong
   C. To overtake Japan as economic superpower
   D. Competition with ASEAN

IV. Asian global relationships
   A. Large trade surpluses
   B. Tourism
   C. Financial markets
   D. Military alliances and modernization
   E. History of Pan-Pacific and Pan-Asian regionalism
   F. Europe, Latin America, Africa

V. Economic and social indicators
   A. Reduction of poverty; pockets remain

　　　　B.　　High levels of education
　　　　C.　　Urbanization
　　　　D.　　Lack of sufficient infrastructure
　　　　E.　　Problems with internal migration
　　　　F.　　High levels of technological development
　　　　G.　　Problems with environmental degradation
　　　　H.　　Attempted control of communication by governments destined to failure
VI.　Values
　　　　A.　　Confucian balance, sacrifice, authority
　　　　B.　　Technology for the benefit of society
　　　　C.　　Support for more equal distribution of consumption

Key Terms

Spreading "V"
APEC
ASEAN
GATT
NIEs

ASEAN Regional Forum (ARF)
special economic zones (SEZ)
export processing zones (EPZ)
Pacific Economic Cooperation Council (PECC)

Key Concepts

region: A region can be defined geographically in terms of land segment, politically in terms of a group of countries, or socially as characterized by cultural affinity.

asymmetry: In the context of this chapter, assymetry refers to an unequal balance of power between and among states.

global trade: trade among the countries of the world, sometimes referred to as trans-national.

intra-regional trade: trade among and between the countries in a region.

direct assistance: financial assistance given in bilateral relationships, that is directly from one country's government to another country's government.

engines of growth: In economic terms, an engine of growth would include any impetus or catalyst in the market which supports sustained economic growth and development

pacifism: a preference for non-war and support for those beliefs and activities which support conflict management and resolution.

hegemony: In the context of contemporary politics, a hegemony is a country who has predominant power relative to other countries.

regional security dialogue: diplomatic exchanges which reference multilateral alliances. In the Pacific region, these conversations may make place among subregional powers, within the context of ASEAN, (or during economic focused meetings of APEC), or in special summit meetings of heads of state.

social indicator: measurements of the well-being of a society which may include education, health, welfare, longevity, infant mortality, caloric intake, housing, and women's health.

internal migration: movement of populations within the boundaries of a country. If the population is intentionally displaced or moved as a result of conflict, this may result in internal refugees known formally as Displaced Persons.

Knowledge, understanding and evaluation

1. Technological change and development effects social values, but social values also effect the nature of change. In the case of the Asian countries, technology is seen as an instrument of social betterment for the group as well as for the individual.

2. The organization of business, government and social relationships is more integrated than that of most Western countries.

3. Regional integration in Asia is not focused on either Japan or China but reflects a large number of trading patterns and a variety of relationships. These can be visualized as series of overlapping triangles rather than pyramids.

4. Asian influence and integration with Europe, the United States, Africa and Latin America will continue to grow and develop.

5. Japan has joined and in some cases, supplanted the United States as regional leader and "engine of growth."

6. The effects of World War II are not forgotten by countries in the region. Japan will continue to have a moderate role.

7. China will be increasingly important in the region. The transition of Hong Kong from British rule to separate status within China will be provide China with an window to the world.

8. Military security arrangements will move from the U.S. "security umbrella" to more regionally centered power arrangements.

9. Environmental problems with continue to plague the area.

10. Control of energy sources and costs will be important factors in the future.